The Murder of Jesus

The Murder of Jesus

A Study of How Jesus Died

By
JOHN F. MACARTHUR JR.

WORD PUBLISHING

NASHVILLE

A Thomas Nelson Company

THE MURDER OF JESUS: A STUDY OF HOW JESUS DIED

Published by Word Publishing, a Thomas Nelson Company,
P. O. Box 141000, Nashville, TN 37214.

ISBN 0-8499-1554-6

Printed in the United States of America

01 02 03 04 05 06 BVG 9 8 7 6 5

To Joe and Georgia Aleppo

beloved friends whose
tireless labor for the cause of
Christ is a constant
encouragement to me, and
whose passion for the truth
has knit our hearts together.

❧ Contents

CONTENTS

❧ Introduction

RECENT YEARS have seen an unprecedented interest in the inner workings of our society's justice system. Not so long ago, the notion of bringing live television cameras inside the courtroom was highly controversial. Now we have Court TV, an entire cable channel devoted to nothing but courtroom cameras and criminal justice.

Or sometimes *in*justice. If the presence of television cameras in the courtrooms has made anything clear, it is that the criminal justice system does not always work. More than a billion viewers worldwide watched live televised coverage of the yearlong O. J. Simpson murder trial (1995). In the end, most felt the verdict was an utter miscarriage of justice. (A subsequent civil trial seemed to confirm the injustice of the earlier verdict.) Other televised cases have resulted in similarly controversial verdicts. Here is graphic proof that human courts cannot guarantee ultimate justice.

Even before the advent of cameras in the courtroom, it was clear that the finest courts of earthly jurisprudence sometimes convict the innocent or exonerate the guilty. Take, for example, the case of Randall Dale Adams, who was convicted and sentenced to death in 1977 for the murder of a Texas policeman. A 1988 documentary, *The Thin Blue Line,* raised troubling questions about law enforcement's handling of his case and helped win him a new trial just hours before his scheduled execution in 1988. A year later he was released from prison when the prosecutor in the case dismissed all charges against him, acknowledging the lack of any real evidence to convict him. An even more disturbing case was that of Kirk Bloodsworth, sentenced to death for rape and murder in the 1980s. After nearly a decade on death row, Bloodsworth was released in 1994 when sophisticated DNA tests proved beyond question that he was innocent of the crimes he had been condemned to death for.

More recently, a Los Angeles police officer admitted that he and his partner shot a man they had in custody, leaving him permanently paralyzed. They then planted a weapon in order to frame the man on an assault charge. The victim, Javier Francisco Ovando, was convicted on the basis of that false testimony and sentenced to twenty-three years in prison. He served three years before the truth was discovered. He was released from prison in 1999 when one of the offending officers confessed, but Ovando will be confined to a wheelchair for the rest of his life.

We're rightly appalled and outraged by such cases, and yet they do not appear to be diminishing in number. Nearly every week, it seems some new, gross miscarriage of justice is dissected on *20/20, 60 Minutes, 48 Hours,* or similar network news magazine programs. Americans' confidence in their criminal justice system may be at an all-time low.

Modern society's concern about justice gone awry is nothing new. Notorious cases of innocent victims who were imprisoned or executed wrongfully litter the pages of history, from the biblical account of Naboth, who was framed and executed by Ahab in ancient Israel, to the witchcraft trials of medieval history, right down to the present age. On the other side of the ledger, history is also replete with accounts of guilty people let off scot-free by so-called courts of justice, ranging from ancient aristocrats who routinely got away with murder, to modern organized-crime bosses who use bribery and intimidation to manipulate the system in their favor.

Clearly, real justice has often been elusive in earthly courts. Innocent Joseph languished in a dank prison while his false accuser, Potiphar's wife, lived in Egyptian luxury. Nero set fire to Rome for political purposes and falsely accused Christians of the crime; then he enlisted Roman courts to perpetrate a slaughter against innocent believers, punishing them for an act he himself committed. Medieval clergy lived lives of wanton profligacy while the Church's office of the Inquisition approved the torture and killing of godly people accused of "heresy." With the Supreme Court's sanction, modern abortionists routinely kill infants at birth, while government bureaucrats spend billions to protect snail darters and silverspot butterflies.

Human courts have an uncanny knack for turning justice completely on its head. The wicked frequently prosper while the righteous suffer wrongfully.

Nowhere is this seen more graphically than in the arrest, trials, and crucifixion of Jesus Christ. No victim of injustice was ever more innocent than the sinless Son of God. And yet no one ever suffered more agony than He did. He was cruelly executed by men who openly acknowledged His faultlessness. Yet at the same time Barabbas, a murderous, thieving insurrectionist, was summarily set free. It was the greatest travesty of justice the world will ever see.

Consider the facts: Jesus Christ was the only truly sinless individual who ever lived—the most innocent, blameless, virtuous man of all time. He "committed no sin, nor was deceit found in His mouth" (1 Peter 2:22). He was "holy, harmless, undefiled, separate from sinners" (Hebrews 7:26). And yet the torment and punishment He suffered in His death was infinitely more heinous than anyone else has ever suffered. He bore the full weight of retribution for human evil. He suffered *as if* He were guilty of humanity's worst offenses. And yet He was guilty of nothing.

It is easy to look at the cross and conclude that this was the worst miscarriage of human justice in the history of the world. And it was. It was an evil act, perpetrated by the hands of wicked men.

But that is not the *full* story. The crucifixion of Christ was also the greatest act of divine justice ever carried out. It was done in full accord with "the determined purpose and foreknowledge of God" (Acts 2:23)—and for the highest of purposes: The death of Christ secured the salvation of untold numbers and opened the way for God to forgive sin without compromising His own perfectly holy standard.

Christ was no mere victim of unjust men when He hung on the cross. Though murdered unjustly and illegally by men whose intentions were only evil, Christ died willingly, becoming an atonement for the sins of the very ones who killed Him. It was the greatest sacrifice ever made; the purest act of love ever carried out; and ultimately an infinitely higher act of divine justice than all the human *in*justice it represented.

Every true Christian knows that Christ died for our sins. That truth is so rich that only eternity will reveal its full profundity. But in the mundane existence of our daily lives, we are too inclined to take the Cross of Christ for granted. We mistakenly think of it as one of the elementary facts of our faith. We therefore neglect to meditate on this truth of all truths, and we miss the real richness of it. If we think of it at all, we tend to dabble too much in the shallow end of the pool, when we ought to be immersing ourselves in its depths daily.

Many wrongly think of Christ as merely a victim of human injustice, a martyr who suffered tragically and unnecessarily. But the truth is that His death was God's plan. In fact, it was the key to God's eternal plan of redemption. Far from being an unnecessary tragedy, the death of Christ was a glorious victory—the most gracious and wonderful act divine benevolence ever rendered on behalf of sinners. It is the consummate expression of God's love for them.

Yet here also we see the wrath of God against sin. What is too often missed in all our songs and sermons about the Cross is that it was the outpouring of divine judgment against the person of Christ—not because *He* deserved that judgment, but because He bore it on behalf of those whom He would redeem. In the words of Isaac Watts,

> Did e'er such love and sorrow meet,
> Or thorns compose so rich a crown?

My aim in this book is to examine the biblical account of Christ's arrest, trial, and crucifixion—and in doing so to try to unfold the rich redemptive significance of our Lord's work on the cross.

Christ's death is by far the most important event in human history. It is the focal point of the Christian faith and will be our refuge in the final judgment. Therefore it also ought to be the main sanctuary for every believer's private meditation. All our most precious hopes stem from the Cross of Christ, and therefore our highest thoughts should also be rooted there. It is a subject we can ill afford to neglect or treat lightly. It is the shame of the modern church that our focus is so often fixed elsewhere.

My approach will be to examine the biblical chronicle of crucifixion events as a historical narrative, rather than dealing with the doctrine of the atonement strictly in the manner of a theologian. The scriptural account gives the reader a front-row seat as the drama unfolds around Christ and His disciples. We are thus placed virtually on the scene, confronted up close with the dreadful horror of the cross as well as its majestic glory. The scene set before us is at once shocking and sublime. It is both disturbing and inspiring. My prayer is that as you read you will be gripped not only by the gross miscarriage of human justice, but also by the remarkable wonder of divine justice, which provided salvation for sinners who could never have rescued themselves.

May we never take the Cross of Christ for granted or miss its profundity. It was here that mercy and truth met together; righteousness and peace kissed each other (Psalm 81:10).

1

Then the chief priests, the scribes, and the elders of the people assembled at the palace of the high priest, who was called Caiaphas, and plotted to take Jesus by trickery and kill Him.

—MATTHEW 26:3–4

1

 The Plot to Kill Jesus

WHO KILLED JESUS?

Over the years the Jewish people have usually borne the brunt of the blame. The expression "Christ killers" has often been employed as a racial epithet by misguided zealots and hate-mongers. And sadly, the charge of killing Jesus has frequently been employed to justify everything from hate crimes to holocausts against the Jewish people. Even though these pogroms have sometimes been carried out in the name of Jesus, such bigotry stems from satanic and anti-Christian motives, certainly not from any genuine love of Christ.

There is, however, a true sense in which both Old and New Testaments hold Israel culpable for the murder of her Messiah. Isaiah 49:7, for example, speaks of the Holy One, the coming Messiah, as "Him whom man despises . . . Him whom the nation abhors." Isaiah 53:3 prophetically describes how the Messiah would be despised and not esteemed by His own people, who would, as it were, hide their faces from Him in the hour of His death. Psalm 22:6–8 prophetically describes the treatment Christ would receive at the hands of His own brethren as He hung on the cross: "I am a worm, and no man; a reproach of men, and despised by the people. All those who see Me ridicule Me; they shoot out the lip, they shake the head, saying, 'He trusted in the LORD, let Him rescue Him; let Him deliver Him, since He delights in Him!'"

In the New Testament, we read that the plot to kill Jesus was hatched in a secret council led by none other than Caiaphas, the high priest:

> The chief priests and the Pharisees gathered a council and said, "What shall we do? For this Man works many signs. If we let Him alone like this, everyone will believe in Him, and the Romans will come and take away both our place and nation." And one of them, Caiaphas, being high priest that year, said to them, "You know nothing at all, nor do you consider that it is expedient for us that one man should die for the people, and not that the whole nation should perish.". . . Then, from that day on, they plotted to put Him to death. (John 11:47–50, 53)

That council, which clearly involved the Sanhedrin, the ruling council in Israel during the time of Christ, was certainly culpable. And there is a legitimate sense in which the guilt of the crime was shared not only by the chief priests and rulers, but also by the people of Israel (cf. Luke 23:13). They were the ones who shouted, "Crucify Him, crucify Him!" as He stood on trial before Pilate (v. 21). That is why Peter, speaking in Jerusalem on the day of Pentecost, addressed the "men of Israel" and said, "*You* have taken [Christ] by lawless hands, have crucified [Him], and put [Him] to death" (Acts 2:22–23, emphasis added).

But were the Jews any *more* culpable than others for Christ's death? Certainly not. It was, after all, Pontius Pilate, a Gentile Roman governor, who sentenced Him to death. And he did so in collusion with Herod Antipas, who (although he bore the title "King of the Jews") was no Jew, but rather an Idumean—a foreign ruler, hated by the Jews, whose throne was granted by Caesar.

Furthermore, crucifixion was a Roman method of execution, authorized and carried out by Roman, not Jewish, authorities. Roman soldiers drove the nails through Christ's hands and feet. Roman troops erected the cross (Matthew 27:27–35). A Roman spear pierced His side (John 19:34). Gentile hands therefore played an even more prominent role in the actual murder of Jesus than the Jews did.

In fact, the murder of Jesus was a vast conspiracy involving Rome, Herod, the Gentiles, the Jewish Sanhedrin, and the people of Israel—diverse groups who apart from this event were seldom fully in accord with one another. In fact, it is significant that the crucifixion of Christ is the *only* historical event where all those factions worked together to achieve a common goal. All were culpable. All bear the guilt together. The Jews as a race were no more or less blameworthy than the Gentiles.

This is very plainly stated in Acts 4:27, a corporate prayer offered in an assembly of the very earliest believers: "For of a truth against thy holy child Jesus, whom thou hast anointed, both Herod, and Pontius Pilate, with the Gentiles, and the people of Israel, were gathered together" (KJV). So there is no justification whatsoever for trying to fix the blame for Jesus' death on any one people group. This was, in essence, a corporate act of sinful humanity against God. All are guilty together.

And yet even that does not exhaust the full truth about who killed Jesus. Scripture emphasizes from cover to cover that the death of Christ was ordained and appointed by God Himself.

One of the key Old Testament prophecies about the crucifixion is Isaiah 53. Isaiah prophetically describes the torture of the Messiah at the hands of a scoffing mob, and then adds, "Yet it pleased the LORD to bruise Him; He has put Him to grief" (Isaiah 53:10). God put his own Son to death? That is precisely what Scripture teaches. Why? According to Isaiah 53:10, it was to "make His soul an offering for sin." God had a redemptive purpose.

The designs of those who killed Christ were entirely murderous. They are by no means exonerated from their evil, just because God's purposes are good. It was still the act of "lawless hands" (Acts 2:23). It was, as far as the human perpetrators were concerned, the ultimate act of pure evil. The wickedness of the crucifixion is in no sense mitigated by the fact that God sovereignly ordained it for good. The truth that it was His sovereign plan makes the deed itself no less a diabolical act of murder.

And yet this *was* clearly God's holy and sovereign plan from before the foundation of the world (Revelation 13:8). Look again at that prayer from Acts 4, this time in its full context:

> Lord, You are God, who made heaven and earth and the sea, and all that is in them, who by the mouth of Your servant David have said: "Why did the nations rage, and the people plot vain things? The kings of the earth took their stand, and the rulers were gathered together against the LORD and against His Christ." For truly against Your holy Servant Jesus, whom You anointed, both Herod and Pontius Pilate, with the Gentiles and the people of Israel, were gathered together *to do whatever Your hand and Your purpose determined before to be done.* (Acts 4:24–28, emphasis added)

Acts 2:23 echoes the same thought: "Him, *being delivered by the determined purpose and foreknowledge of God,* you have taken by lawless hands, have crucified, and put to death" (emphasis added).

God ordained the murder of Jesus. Or to put it starkly in the words of Isaiah 53:10, it *pleased* the Lord to bruise Him.

In what sense was God pleased by the death of His Son?

He was pleased by the redemption that was accomplished. He was pleased that His eternal plan of salvation was thus fulfilled. He was pleased with the sacrifice of His Son, who died so that others might have eternal life. He was pleased to display His righteous anger against sin in such a graphic way. He was pleased to demonstrate His love for sinners through such a majestic sacrifice.

For all the evil in the crucifixion, it brought about an infinite good. In fact, here was the most evil act ever perpetrated by sinful hearts: The sinless Son of God—holy God Himself in human flesh—was unjustly killed after being subjected to the most horrific tortures that could be devised by wicked minds. It was the evil of all evils, the worst deed human depravity could ever devise, and the most vile evil that has ever been committed. And yet from it came the greatest good of all time—the redemption of unnumbered souls, and the demonstration of the glory of God as Savior. Though the murderers meant evil against Christ, God meant it for good, in order to save many (cf. Genesis 50:20).

The Cross is therefore the ultimate proof of the utter sovereignty of God. His purposes are always fulfilled in spite of the evil intentions of sinners. God even works His righteousness *through* the evil acts of unrighteous agents. Far from making Him culpable for their evil, this demonstrates how all He does is good, and how He is able to work all things together for good (Romans 8:28)—even the most wicked deed the powers of evil have ever conspired to carry out.

Furthermore, if God was sovereignly in control when the unlawful hands of murderous men put His beloved Son on a cross, why would anyone balk at the notion that God is still sovereignly in control even when lesser evils occur? The Cross therefore establishes God's absolute sovereignty beyond question.

THE CONSPIRACY IS BORN

The drama of the crucifixion begins in Matthew 26, where the plot to murder Jesus is hatched. Actually, in a very important sense, the entire life of Christ had been a prologue to this moment. He condescended to become a man with the express purpose of dying (John 12:27; Philippians 2:4–7; Hebrews 2:14). As He stood before Pilate to be condemned to death, Christ Himself said, "For this cause I was born, and for this cause I have come into the world" (John 18:37). He repeatedly spoke of the hour of His death as "my hour" (John 2:4; 7:6, 30; 8:20; 12:23; 13:1; 17:1). Everything in His life was preparation for the hour of His death.

Jesus had told His disciples numerous times that He would die at the hands of those who hated Him. In fact, long before His final journey to Jerusalem, "while they were staying in Galilee, Jesus said to them, 'The Son of Man is about to be betrayed into the hands of men, and they will kill Him'" (Matthew 17:22–23; cf. 16:21; 20:17–19).

Now the hour had come, and an unstoppable chain of events had begun that would end in His murder. His final week of earthly ministry was drawing to a close. Christ had just finished His Olivet Discourse, the great prophetic sermon that spans Matthew 24–25. But His thoughts were not far from the subject of His death. Matthew writes, "Now it came to pass, when Jesus had finished all these sayings, that He said to His disciples, 'You know that after two days is the Passover, and the Son of Man will be delivered up to be crucified'" (26:1–2). He knew His hour had come. The sovereign plan of God for the redemption of sinners was about to come to fruition. And although evil men were at that very moment plotting His death in secret, it was no secret from the sovereign, omniscient mind of Christ.

Only a few days before, He rode into the city in triumph, while shouts of "Hosanna" rang from crowds lining the streets. To the disciples—to any observant human eye—it looked as if He would be swept onto the Messianic throne with an unstoppable wave of grass-roots support. But Jesus knew the real truth. Public opinion is fickle. Righteousness will never triumph through public opinion anyway. The fawning masses were attracted to Jesus' miracles, but they were not prepared to acknowledge their sin and yield to Him as Lord. It is entirely probable that many of the same people who were shouting hosannas to Him at the beginning of the week were the same ones yelling "Crucify Him, crucify Him!" before the week was over.

Nonetheless, the Jewish leaders, threatened by Jesus' apparent popularity among the people of Jerusalem, met together clandestinely to discuss what to do about Him. Matthew describes the scene: "Then the chief priests, the scribes, and the elders of the people assembled at the palace of the high priest, who was called Caiaphas, and plotted to take Jesus by trickery and kill Him. But they said, 'Not during the feast, lest there be an uproar among the people'" (Matthew 26:3–5).

The evil plot would ultimately succeed, but only in accord with the divine plan, and only according to the divine timetable. In fact, had the murder of Jesus not been part of the eternal plan of God, it would never have happened. Jesus said of His Life, "No one takes it from Me, but I lay it down of Myself. I have power to lay it down, and I have power to take it again. This command I have received from My Father" (John 10:18). Pilate would attempt to force Jesus to answer the accusations against Him by citing his own authority as governor—"Do You not know that I have power to crucify You, and power to release You?" (John 19:10). But Jesus replied, "You could have no power at all against Me unless it had been given you from above" (v. 11). Clearly, God was utterly sovereign in every aspect of what was occurring.

In fact, on several occasions prior to this, various enemies of Christ had sought to kill Him but were divinely thwarted because it was not yet His time. The earliest attempt to kill Him was immediately after His birth. Herod slaughtered all the male infants in and around Bethlehem, because he heard the Messiah had been born there. But an angel from the Lord warned Joseph, and the little family fled to Egypt until the threat had passed.

In one of his first acts of public ministry, Christ read from the scroll of Isaiah in His hometown synagogue in Nazareth. The people became so enraged at His teaching when He claimed to be the One who the prophet wrote about that they carried Him out of the city to the brow of the hill on which the city stood. Their plan was to throw Him off the cliff to His death, but He supernaturally eluded them (Luke 4:16–30). It was not yet His time.

During Christ's earlier ministry in Jerusalem, He healed a man at the pool of Bethesda on the Sabbath. When the religious leaders challenged Him, Christ replied that His Father was working, so it was fitting for Him to work as well (John 5:17). John writes, "The Jews sought all the more to kill Him, because He not only broke the Sabbath, but also said that God was His Father, making Himself equal with God" (v. 18). Many of those same Jewish leaders were no doubt the same ones who later would join the plot with Caiaphas.

During that earlier time of ministry in Jerusalem, it became so well known that the Jewish leaders were seeking to kill Jesus that He was referred to as "He whom they seek to kill" (John 7:25). The widespread knowledge that His life was in danger did not deter Jesus in the least. He continued speaking boldly, and the Jewish leaders, intimidated by His fearlessness, said nothing to Him. That caused many people to wonder if the Sanhedrin *knew* He was the Messiah (v. 26). Even the temple guard, assigned to arrest Him, cowered at His boldness. When the chief priests and Pharisees demanded to know why He had not been arrested, the temple officers replied, "No man ever spoke like this Man!" (John 7:46).

It was not yet His time, and not until His time had come could their murderous plans possibly succeed.

When it *was* His time, He knew it. On the night of His arrest, He told the disciples, "The Son of Man goes as it has been determined" (Luke 22:22).

And so the plot that was being devised against Jesus by His enemies was in perfect accord with the plan of God from eternity past.

The apostle John underscores that fact in his account of the conspirators' private discussions. John may have obtained details about what was said at the meeting from someone actually present when the conspiracy was being planned—probably Nicodemus, who is identified as a ruler of the Jews (John 3:1), yet seems to have been secretly sympathetic to Christ (cf. John 7:50–51; 19:38–39). John reports that the Jewish leaders were fearful that Christ's popularity among the people would result in pressure to recognize Him as Messiah and rightful ruler of the Jews. That would disrupt the uneasy peace with Rome, and it would enflame the anti-Roman Zealots, a rogue political faction who wanted to overthrow Roman rule. That in turn would pose a threat to the status of the high priest and Sanhedrin, who wielded a token authority in Jewish society (especially in religious affairs) by permission of Rome (John 11:48). The Jewish leaders were therefore doing all they could to quell messianic fervor in Israel. Moreover, Pilate was already responding to Jewish Zealotry by suppressing it with violence (cf. Luke 13:1). So the Jewish leaders concluded that they *had* to silence Jesus, without regard to whether He was the true Messiah or not.

The leading character in this scene is Caiaphas, the high priest that year. Caiaphas was a politically motivated, pragmatic opportunist. Biblically, of course, the high priesthood was passed through the Levitical line. During the Roman occupation, however, high priests were approved and appointed by Rome. Historical evidence strongly suggests that the office was often purchased with money or granted as a political favor. Caiaphas had married the daughter of Annas, former high priest (John 18:13). Annas still wielded significant power through his son-in-law, so that the office amounted to a kind of joint priesthood (Luke 3:2). History records that Caiaphas held the office for more than two decades—an extraordinarily long time when we consider that in a hundred years of Roman occupation, twenty-eight men served as high priest. (When Caiaphas was finally deposed from the high priesthood in A.D. 36–37 by the Roman governor Vitellus, his successor lasted a mere fifty days.) The length of Caiaphas's tenure suggests that he had somehow gained unusual favor with Rome. He was certainly corrupt. It was under his authority that the moneychangers plied their trade on the temple grounds. This had no doubt made him an extremely wealthy man. And given the fact that Christ had twice driven the moneychangers from the temple (John 2:14–16; Matthew 21:12–13), it is no wonder Caiaphas hated Him so much.

Caiaphas was a Sadducee. The Sadducees were an aristocratic sect who controlled the temple in Jesus' time. They were religious liberals and utter materialists, denying the resurrection of the dead, heaven, angels, and all the supernatural elements of Scripture (Acts 23:8). They interpreted the law of Moses with a rigorous literalism but tended to discount or downplay the rest of Scripture. They were therefore normally in opposition to the Pharisees, but the two groups had often conspired together to try to discredit Christ, and in each case He had silenced and embarrassed them (Matthew 16:1–4; 22:34–35; Mark 12:13–23). Now they were united once more in the plot to kill Him.

It was Caiaphas who said, "It is expedient for us that one man should die for the people, and not that the whole nation should perish" (John 11:50). Although Caiaphas was talking about murdering Jesus to suppress a political threat, John saw an unintentional prophetic significance in his words: "Now this he did not say on his own authority; but being high priest that year he prophesied that Jesus would die for the nation, and not for that nation only, but also that He would gather together in one the children of God who were scattered abroad" (vv. 51–52).

In other words, what Caiaphas and the Sanhedrin were planning for evil reasons, God intended for good (cf. Genesis 50:20). They wanted to kill Jesus in order to save the nation from the immediate threat of violent destruction at the hands of Rome. God was willing to sacrifice His Son in order to save the nation—indeed, people from *every* nation—from eternal condemnation because of their sin. The apostle John would employ almost identical language in a later epistle, "He Himself is the propitiation for our sins, and not for ours only but also for the whole world" (1 John 2:2).

And thus the evil plans of these conspirators coincided precisely with the eternal plan of God.

The timing was also in precise accord with the plan of God. It was Passover, when the sacrificial lambs were slain. And Christ was to be "the Lamb of God who takes away the sin of the world" (John 1:29). He was the divine fulfillment of what Passover had always foreshadowed. "He was oppressed and He was afflicted, yet He opened not His mouth; He was led as a lamb to the slaughter, and as a sheep before its shearers is silent, so He opened not His mouth" (Isaiah 53:7; cf. Acts 8:32).

Notice that the scheme of the Sanhedrin was "to take Jesus by trickery and kill Him. But they said, 'Not during the feast, lest there be an uproar among the people'" (Matthew 26:4–5). They no doubt hoped to kill Him with as little fanfare as possible, and therefore they resolved to wait until the Passover season was over and Jerusalem would be less crowded. Their concern for avoiding the feast was not to preserve the sanctity of the feast (for criminals were often executed during the feasts, precisely because there were more witnesses at those times). But they wanted to avoid public scrutiny, and above all they did not want to provoke a public uproar.

This again reveals the sovereignty of God over the schemes of men. They wanted to avoid a public scandal on the feast day; God's design was for Christ to die on Passover, in as public a manner as possible. "There are many plans in a man's heart, nevertheless the Lord's counsel—that will stand" (Proverbs 19:21). "Who is he who speaks and it comes to pass, when the Lord has not commanded it?" (Lamentations 3:37).

Jerusalem was crowded with pilgrims from every corner of the empire who had come to celebrate the Passover. The historian Josephus estimated that more than a quarter-million sacrificial lambs would be slain in Jerusalem during a typical Passover season. On average, ten people would partake of one lamb, suggesting that the Jewish population in Jerusalem during Passover could swell to between 2.5 and 3 million. Even the Roman governor, Pontius Pilate (whose headquarters were in the coastal town of Caesarea) came to Jerusalem during the Passover. From the conspirators' perspective, it was the worst time to seize Jesus, if they wanted to do it quietly. They had seen Him receive adulation from the crowds, and they knew they risked provoking a riot.

But Passover was *His* time—the time God had chosen, the time most fitting for the Lamb of God to die for the sins of the world. And the conspiracy would ultimately be carried out according to God's timing, not Caiaphas's. Always before, when the conspirators had tried to kill Jesus prior to His time, God had thwarted their plans. Now that they wanted to delay until a more expedient time, they could not postpone the perfect timing of God.

CHRIST IS ANOINTED FOR HIS BURIAL

Matthew includes a touching vignette that further displays God's sovereign control of the events leading up to the crucifixion. It stands in stark contrast to the conspiracy being plotted in the palace of the high priest. There, men who hated Jesus plotted His demise. Here, a woman who loved Him prepares Him for burial:

And when Jesus was in Bethany at the house of Simon the leper, a woman came to Him having an alabaster flask of very costly fragrant oil, and she poured it on His head as He sat at the table. But when His disciples saw it, they were indignant, saying, "Why this waste? For this fragrant oil might have been sold for much and given to the poor." But when Jesus was aware of it, He said to them, "Why do you trouble the woman? For she has done a good work for Me. For you have the poor with you always, but Me you do not have always. For in pouring this fragrant oil on My body, she did it for My burial. Assuredly, I say to you, wherever this gospel is preached in the whole world, what this woman has done will also be told as a memorial to her." (Matthew 26:6–13)

Matthew included this account at this point in his narrative because of its relevance to his subject. Chronologically, however, it pertains to the events of the previous Sabbath (John 12:1–3)— when Jesus was in Bethany and Bethphage (on the eastern outskirts of Jerusalem), preparing for his triumphal entry into the city the following day. That evening, Christ and the disciples were invited to dinner in the home of Simon the leper. We know nothing of Simon other than what is recorded here, but it is evident that he was someone whom Christ had healed of leprosy, for no one with an active case of leprosy would have been serving such a banquet. The evening was probably arranged as an expression of Simon's gratitude for the Lord's grace to him.

The apostle John describes this same event, and informs us that Mary, Martha, and Lazarus were present, with Martha serving the meal and Lazarus sitting at the table (John 12:1–2). The three were no doubt friends of Simon, possibly close neighbors, because Bethany was their hometown too.

It was Mary who anointed Christ with the perfume (v. 3). John says she anointed not only His head, but also His feet, and wiped His feet with her hair. She was probably deliberately emulating the forgiven prostitute described in Luke 7:36–39, who also anointed Jesus' feet with fragrant oil and wiped His feet with her hair. That anointing occurred in Galilee, at the home of a Pharisee, at an earlier time in Christ's ministry. Mary, a close follower of Christ, no doubt knew of the incident and, being touched by the pure worship that motivated that woman's gesture, did the same thing herself, with the costliest fragrance she could buy.

Both John 12:5 and Mark 14:5 record that the ointment was worth three hundred denarii—about a year's wages for the typical laborer. It came in an alabaster flask, also very expensive, and Mark records that Mary broke the flask (v. 3), thus making her sacrificial act that much more lavish.

The disciples were indignant. Mary's liberality seemed over-extravagant to them. After all, they reasoned, the ointment could have been sold and the proceeds given to the poor. John's account informs us that Judas was the ringleader in voicing this sentiment. His concern was hardly as noble as he tried to make it sound. "This he said, not that he cared for the poor, but because he was a thief, and had the money box; and he used to take what was put in it" (John 12:6).

It is significant that Judas was the group's treasurer. This reveals how trusted he was (cf. Psalm 41:9). And the fact that the others followed his lead in this instance reveals that he had gained not only their trust but also to a very large degree, their respect. Evidently, none of the other disciples ever suspected he would become a traitor, because even when Jesus prophesied that He would be betrayed by one of them, not one person pointed the finger at Judas. They all seemed to doubt themselves more than they doubted Judas (Mark 14:19).

It is typical of the spirit of Judas that he did not voice his displeasure about Mary's act aloud in front of Jesus. According to Mark, the disciples first discussed the matter privately among themselves, and then they took their complaint—framed as a sharp rebuke—to Mary (Mark 14:4–5).

Though they evidently had tried to conceal their displeasure from Jesus, He knew. And He rebuked them for their murmuring against her: "Let her alone" (John 12:6).

If He were not God in human flesh, worthy of such an act of

worship—and about to die for others' sins—the rest of His reply might seem cold and inhumane: "For you have the poor with you always, but Me you do not have always" (Matthew 26:11). Those were unusual-sounding words from the lips of the Savior, who had, after all, commanded the rich young ruler to sell all his possessions and give to the poor (Matthew 19:21).

But here Jesus was merely echoing a truth contained in Moses' law: "The poor will never cease from the land; therefore I command you, saying, 'You shall open your hand wide to your brother, to your poor and your needy, in your land'" (Deuteronomy 15:11). Liberality to the poor is our *constant* obligation, and Jesus was not diminishing, but underscoring, the importance of it. At *that* moment, however, there was a higher need to be met than earthly poverty. Christ was about to die. He was nearing the end of his earthly ministry. He had told them this already. Soon they would have Him with them no more.

Mary, who had always been more attentive than most to the teaching of Christ (Luke 10:39), may have understood more than the others. She evidently sensed that Christ was at a major turning point in His earthly ministry. Whether this meant she fully understood that He was about to die is not entirely clear. It seems unlikely that Mary was consciously aware that Christ's death was so near at hand. She probably intended her gesture simply as an act of profound worship.

But there was a symbolic significance to the act that had been sovereignly designed by God Himself. Jesus said, "For in pouring this fragrant oil on My body, she did it for My burial" (Matthew 26:12). And so again we see the sovereign hand of God in orchestrating every event that unfolds. Mary's gesture of love and worship to Christ was, more significantly, a divinely ordained symbolic act of preparation for His death and burial. It was, in a sense, a token of love from the Father to the Son, signifying that now was His time.

THE TRAITOR MAKES HIS DEAL

It may well be that Christ's rebuke on that occasion sealed what had been a growing disillusionment in Judas's mind. He may have been questioning the Messianic credentials of Jesus. After all, like nearly everyone else, he expected a Messiah who would deliver Israel from Roman oppression and establish His throne. Judas (as well as the other disciples) no doubt had hoped to share in the glory and power of that kingdom (cf. Matthew 20:20–21). But as Jesus talked more and more about His rejection and impending death, Judas lost enthusiasm for following Him. He had hung on for three years hoping Jesus would take the throne of David and elevate him. His motives all along appear to have been greed and a selfish thirst for power.

Combine that with the fact that he was pilfering from the disciples' treasury, which he was responsible for. He watched with resentment as such costly gifts—a pound of pure spikenard and an alabaster flask—were sacrificed in an act of sheer worship. And as Judas saw the potential profits of a planned embezzlement evaporate, he may have decided then and there to make up for the loss by selling Jesus. And thus it may have been at this very moment that he made his final decision to commit an act of treachery by handing Jesus over to His enemies.

Luke records that Satan himself entered into Judas at about this time (Luke 22:3). Operating through Judas's greed, and taking advantage of an unregenerate heart that had by now utterly spurned Jesus, the devil literally possessed Judas to carry out the act of treachery that was about to occur. For Judas's part, when he turned from Christ in this final act of rejection, he willingly gave himself over to the control of the powers of darkness, and become a tool of Satan. Matthew tells us, "Then one of the twelve, called Judas Iscariot, went to the chief priests and said, 'What are you willing to give me if I deliver Him to you?' And they counted out to him thirty pieces of silver. So from that time he sought opportunity to betray Him" (Matthew 26:14–16).

Judas may even have gone to the house of Caiaphas in the exact hour the Sanhedrin were meeting there to plan their own conspiracy against Jesus. In any case, Judas's treacherous plans perfectly melded with theirs, and they immediately weighed out the betrayal price and paid him.

It was the price of a slave—thirty pieces of silver (Exodus 21:32). These were probably silver shekels. Thirty shekels would be worth about 120 denarii—less than the value of Mary's spikenard. Judas may have even deluded himself into thinking there was some justice in this act as a response to what he had convinced himself was an act of wanton extravagance.

The Sanhedrin no doubt took special pleasure in the fact that they were assisted in their plot by one of Jesus' closest disciples. They may have also imagined that this somehow vindicated their evil plans.

And from that point on, Judas looked for an opportunity to betray Jesus. Having already accepted money for the deed, he was irrevocably committed. Now all he had to do was select an occasion when Jesus was alone, or nearly so, in order to fit into the Sanhedrin's plans to capture Jesus quietly. And he ultimately decided that the best opportunity would be in the garden where Jesus often went to pray alone with His closest friends.

From an earthly perspective, it appeared that the schemes of Jesus' enemies were beginning to come together perfectly. The

Sanhedrin were no doubt thrilled to have added a conspirator from Jesus' own inner circle. Judas was undoubtedly pleased to have profited so neatly from his treachery. From His opponents' standpoint, things were falling together nicely.

No one but Jesus Himself realized it at the time, but a higher plan was really at work. It was the eternal plan of a sovereign God—a plan that had been laid out from before the foundation of the world. And from the very inception of the plot, the fact of God's sovereign control is made clear by all the prophecies that were fulfilled as the drama unfolds perfectly in accord with God's eternal purposes. Thus the first and most basic lesson we gain from the murder of Jesus is the truth that God remains absolutely sovereign over all, even when it seems the most evil schemes of sinful men are about to achieve a sinister success.

2

The Teacher says, "My time is at hand; I will keep the Passover . . . with My disciples."

—MATTHEW 26:18

2

⚜ The Last Passover

PASSOVER WAS THE FIRST FEAST of the Jewish calendar, held every year "on the fourteenth day of the first month at twilight" (Leviticus 23:5). It was then that every family in Israel commemorated the nation's deliverance from Egypt with the sacrifice of a spotless lamb. The feast was also the oldest of all the Jewish holy days, the first Passover having been celebrated on the eve of Israel's deliverance from Egypt.

Passover was immediately followed by the feast of Unleavened Bread (Leviticus 23:6). This was a week-long affair, making the entire period of feasting eight days long. The two feasts were so closely associated that the eight-day period was sometimes called "the Passover" and sometimes called "the Feast of Unleavened Bread." (The New Testament itself sometimes uses the terms interchangeably, echoing the common parlance.) But in technical terms, "Passover" refers to the fourteenth of Nisan (first month of the Jewish calendar), and "the Feast of Unleavened Bread" refers to the remaining seven days of the feast season, which ended on 21 Nisan.

Four days prior to Passover, on 10 Nisan, each family in Israel was to select a spotless sacrificial lamb and separate that lamb from the rest of the herds until Passover, when the lamb was to be slain (Exodus 12:3–6). During that final week before His crucifixion, Jesus Himself would undoubtedly have done this with His disciples, selecting a lamb on Monday of that week.

Remember, historical records of Jesus' time indicate that as many as a quarter-million lambs were slain in a typical Passover season, requiring hundreds of priests to carry out the task. Since all the lambs were killed during a two-hour period just before twilight on 14 Nisan (Exodus 12:6), it would have required about six hundred priests, killing an average of four lambs per minute, to accomplish the task in a single evening. Tradition permitted no more than two men to bring a lamb to the temple for sacrifice, and after each lamb was slain, it was to be immediately taken home and roasted. Even so, the temple mount would have been densely crowded while the lambs were being slain, with as many as half a million people moving through the area in a two-hour span.

The Jews of Jesus' day had two different methods of reckoning the calendar, however, and this helped alleviate the problem. The Pharisees, as well as the Jews from Galilee and the northern districts of Israel, counted their days from sunrise to sunrise. But the Sadducees, and people from Jerusalem and the surrounding districts, calculated days from sundown to sundown. That meant 14 Nisan for a Galilean fell on Thursday, while 14 Nisan for the inhabitants of Jerusalem fell on Friday. And thus the slaughter of the lambs could take place in two two-hour time periods on successive days, thereby easing the work of the priests somewhat. About half the lambs could be killed on Thursday, and the other half were killed on Friday.

(That twist in the chronology explains why Jesus and His disciples—all Galileans, except for Judas—ate the Passover meal on Thursday evening in the Upper Room, yet John 18:28 records that the Jewish leaders—all residents of Jerusalem—had not yet celebrated Passover on the following day when Jesus was taken to His trial in the Praetorium. It also explains why John 19:14 indicates that Jesus' trial and crucifixion took place on the day of Preparation for the Passover.)

Still, the amount of blood resulting from all those sacrifices was enormous. The blood was permitted to flow off the steep eastern slope of the temple mount and into the Kidron Valley, where it turned the brook bright crimson for a period of several days. It was a graphic reminder of the awful price of sin.

Of course, all that blood and all those animals could not actually atone for sin. "For it is not possible that the blood of bulls and goats could take away sins" (Hebrews 10:4). The lambs only symbolized a more perfect sacrifice that God Himself would provide to take away sins. That is why John the Baptist looked beyond those animal sacrifices and pointed to the true "Lamb of God who takes away the sin of the world" (John 1:29). The full meaning of that prophecy was about to be unveiled.

THE LAST PASSOVER PREPARED

Early on that Thursday the disciples began their preparation for the Passover Seder. "Now on the first day of the Feast of the Unleavened Bread [here Matthew was employing the common colloquialism that combined the two great feasts] the disciples came to Jesus, saying to Him, 'Where do You want us to prepare for You to eat the Passover?'" (Matthew 26:17).

It is evident from Matthew's account that Jesus had already

prearranged many of the details for the evening. With so many visiting Israelites coming annually to Jerusalem for the feast, it was common for the city's inhabitants to keep rooms that they let out so that visitors could have a private place to eat the Passover meal with friends and family. Jesus had evidently arranged for the use of one such venue for Himself and the disciples—an upper room, probably made available by someone whom Jesus knew and who in turn was a believer in Jesus, but perhaps unknown to the disciples. He is never identified by name in any of the gospel accounts. In any case, Jesus had evidently made these arrangements secretly, to avoid having it known in advance where He would be that evening with the disciples. (If Judas had previously known the location of the Last Supper, it would have been a simple matter for him to reveal to the Sanhedrin where they could find Jesus. But it was necessary in the plan of God for Him to celebrate the Passover with His disciples before His betrayal.)

Many preparations needed to be made. Not only would the lamb need to be slaughtered at the temple and then brought back for roasting, but other elements of the meal also needed to be prepared. Chief among the elements of a Passover Seder were unleavened bread, wine, and a dish made of bitter herbs. The responsibility for preparing these elements was probably divided among a few of the disciples. And the task of arranging the room and the table was already being seen to by a servant of the man who owned the upper room.

So Jesus told them, "Go into the city to a certain man, and say to him, 'The Teacher says, "My time is at hand; I will keep the Passover at your house with My disciples"'" (Matthew 26:18). According to Mark 14:13 and Luke 22:10, Jesus told them the man they were seeking would be "carrying a pitcher of water." Normally, carrying water was a woman's task, so the man would be easy to identify.

Jesus, who knew all things (John 16:30), knew precisely where the man would be when they found Him. This is yet another proof that He was sovereignly in control of all these events.

We learn from Luke 22:8 that it was Peter and John who were specifically assigned to find the man and help prepare the Upper Room. Mark says they were to locate the man, follow him home, and then repeat to the owner of the house what Jesus had told them. There they would find "a large upper room, furnished, and prepared" (Mark 14:15). They "did as Jesus had directed them; and they prepared the Passover" (Matthew 26:19).

There is profound significance in Jesus' statement, "My time is at hand; I will keep the Passover" (v. 18). On several prior occasions, Peter and John had heard Him say, "My time has not yet come" (John 7:6)—or words to that effect. His time was now at hand, the moment He had come into the world for, and He stated that fact plainly for Peter and John. He knew He had one remaining evening to spend with His disciples, and He would spend it keeping the Passover. The Greek expression translated "I will keep the Passover" employs a present-tense expression to express a future event (literally, "I keep the Passover"). Thus He underscored the absolute inviolability of the divinely orchestrated plan.

It was vital for Christ to keep this last Passover. Later that evening He would tell the disciples, "With fervent desire I have desired to eat this Passover with you before I suffer; for I say to you, I will no longer eat of it until it is fulfilled in the kingdom of God" (Luke 22:15–16). The events of that evening would usher in the culmination of everything all previous Passovers had prefigured. The true Lamb of God was about to be sacrificed, and this last Passover meal would therefore be rich with significance, more so than any Passover Seder ever held by the most devout of Jewish families.

THE FEAST EATEN

About the remaining events of that day—right up to the Passover meal itself—the gospel accounts are utterly silent. Jesus may have spent the day alone in prayer with the Father while the disciples prepared for the Passover. Whatever activities consumed the day, Jesus and His disciples met together at the appointed time and went to the Upper Room, where things were fully prepared. The apostle John devotes several chapters (John 13–17) to a detailed recounting of Jesus' Discourse that night. (A full exposition of the Upper Room Discourse is beyond the scope of this current work, but I have dealt with it in another volume.)[1]

Matthew jumps directly to the Upper Room and the scene at the Passover meal. "When evening had come, He sat down with the twelve" (Matthew 26:20). It would have been after 6:00 on Thursday evening when they sat down to the meal. The Greek word translated "sat down" is the verb *anakeimai,* which also means "to recline." It was common to serve a meal like this on a low table, at which guests reclined in order to partake. From John's account, we learn that Christ and the disciples were eating from a reclining position, because John's head was positioned next to Jesus' chest (John 21:20).

This was in stark contrast to the first Passover, which was eaten in haste from a standing position, clothes girded up for travel, sandals on the feet, and staffs in hand (Exodus 12:11). On that occasion, the Israelites were preparing for their escape from Egypt. On this occasion no escape was planned. Christ would go from here to the garden, where He would be betrayed into the hands of His killers. His time was at hand.

There was a well-established sequence for the eating of a Passover Seder. A cup of wine was distributed first, the first of four cups shared during the meal. Each person would take a sip from a common cup. Before the cup was passed, Jesus gave thanks (Luke 22:17).

After the initial cup was passed, there was a ceremonial washing to symbolize the need for moral and spiritual cleansing. It seems to have been during the ceremonial washing that "a dispute [arose] among them, as to which of them should be considered the greatest" (Luke 22:24). John records that Jesus "rose from supper and laid aside His garments, took a towel and girded Himself. After that, He poured water into a basin and began to wash the disciples' feet, and to wipe them with the towel with which He was girded" (John 13:4–5). Taking the role of the lowest servant, Christ thus transformed the washing ceremony into a graphic lesson about humility and true holiness. External washing avails nothing if the heart is defiled. And pride is a sure proof of the need for heart-cleansing. Christ had made a similar point with the Pharisees in Matthew 23:25–28. Now He washed the disciples' feet, illustrating that even believers with regenerate hearts need periodic washing from the external defilement of the world.

His act was a model of true humility. Foot washing was a task typically delegated to the lowest slave. Normally in a hired banquet room like this, an attendant would be provided to wash guests' feet when they entered. To omit this detail was considered a gross discourtesy (cf. Luke 7:44). Foot washing was necessary because of the dust and mud and other filth one encountered as a pedestrian on the unpaved roads in and around Jerusalem. But evidently there was no servant to perform the task when Jesus and the disciples arrived at the Upper Room, so instead of humbling themselves to perform such a demeaning task for one another, the disciples had simply left their feet unwashed. Christ's gesture was both a touching act of self-abasement and a subtle rebuke to the disciples (cf.

John 13:6–9). It was also a pattern for the kind of humility He expects of all Christians (v. 15; cf. Luke 22:25–26).

After the ceremonial washing, the Passover meal continued with the eating of the bitter herbs (Exodus 12:8). (These were parsley, endive, and similar leafy greens.) The bitterness of the herbs evoked the harshness of Israel's bondage in Egypt. The herbs were eaten with pieces of unleavened bread, dipped in a substance called *charoseth*, a chutney made of pomegranates, apples, dates, figs, raisins, and vinegar. The *charoseth* was likened to the mortar used by a bricklayer—and again it was reminiscent of the Israelites' slavery in Egypt, where they made bricks.

Next, the second cup was passed. It was at this point that the head of the household (in this case, it was no doubt Jesus) explained the meaning of Passover (cf. Exodus 12:26–27). In a traditional Jewish Passover Seder, the youngest child asks four prearranged questions, and the answers are recited from a poetic narrative of the Exodus.

The passing of the second cup would be accompanied by the singing of psalms. Traditionally, the psalms sung at Passover were from the *Hallel* (Hebrew for "praise"; this is the same word from which *Hallelujah* is derived). The Hallel consisted of six psalms beginning with Psalm 113. The Hallel psalms were probably sung in order, the first two being sung at this point in the ceremony.

The roasted lamb would be served next. The head of the household would also ceremonially wash his hands again, and he would break and distribute pieces of the unleavened bread to each person around the table, to be eaten with the lamb.

THE EVIL DEED FORETOLD

It probably was at some point in these early stages of the meal—possibly while the lamb was being eaten—that Jesus sounded an ominous note. "Now as they were eating, He said, 'Assuredly, I say to you, one of you will betray Me'" (Matthew 26:21). Several times prior to this He had foretold His own death. This was the first time, however, that He had spoken of being betrayed by one of His own disciples.

One can only imagine what a damper this would have put on what was—for the most part until now—a festive occasion. The word for "betray" is the Greek verb *paradidōmai*, which spoke of handing a prisoner over for punishment. It is the same word used in Matthew 4:12, when John the Baptist was cast into prison. This was an unimaginable thought for most of the disciples—that Jesus would be surrendered to His enemies by one of them. And yet, each evidently knew that the *potential* for such treachery lay within their own hearts. "They were exceedingly sorrowful, and each of them began to say to Him, 'Lord, is it I?'" (Matthew 26:22).

Saying nothing to allay their fears, but underscoring the hideous nature of the treason that was about to take place, Jesus replied, "He who dipped his hand with Me in the dish will betray Me" (v. 23). The gross evil inherent in such hypocrisy and betrayal was perfectly described in one of David's psalms:

> For it is not an enemy who reproaches me;
> Then I could bear it.
> Nor is it one who hates me who has exalted himself
> against me;
> Then I could hide from him.
> But it was you, a man my equal,
> My companion and my acquaintance.
> We took sweet counsel together,
> And walked to the house of God in the throng.

PSALM 55:12–14

In Psalm 41:9, David wrote a similar lament about his trusted counselor Ahithophel, who joined Absalom's rebellion against David: "Even my own familiar friend in whom I trusted, who ate my bread, has lifted up his heel against me."

According to John 13:18, Jesus quoted Psalm 41:9 that night in the Upper Room, indicating that the psalm had a Messianic significance that was about to be fulfilled.

The betrayal of Christ, like every other detail of the crucifixion drama, was part of God's eternal plan of redemption. Jesus acknowledged that fact when He said, "The Son of Man indeed goes just as it is written of Him" (Matthew 26:24). God would use Judas's act of treachery to bring about the redemption of untold multitudes. And yet the act of betrayal itself was not thereby rendered a good thing. Just because God uses an evil act for His own holy purposes, the evil itself cannot therefore be called good. The fact that God's sovereign purposes are always good did not somehow sanctify Judas's evil intentions. Contrary to what some have suggested, Judas was a willing devil (John 6:70), not an unwitting saint. His destiny was eternal damnation. And Christ underscored that truth in Matthew 26:24 as well: "The Son of Man indeed goes just as it is written of Him, but woe to that man by whom the Son of Man is betrayed! It would have been good for that man if he had not been born."

The eleven disciples besides Judas were appalled by the thought that one of their own number would be guilty of such a sinister act. And yet it is notable that their first response was not finger-pointing but self-examination. Having been so recently rebuked by Christ for their lack of humility because of their failure to wash one another's feet, they were no doubt still pondering their own sinful frailty. Now they were made to face an even more troubling prospect: Among this close-knit band of men who trusted one another implicitly, there was a betrayer. Each one examined his own heart, and knowing their own susceptibility to sinful blundering, they anxiously asked Jesus, "Is it I?" Each probably wondered if somehow he might unwittingly do something to jeopardize the Lord or tip off His enemies about where He could be found.

John records, "The disciples looked at one another, perplexed about whom He spoke" (John 13:22). Again, there was nothing in either Judas's behavior or Jesus' treatment of him up to this point that would have given the other disciples a clue that Judas was the betrayer. Although "Jesus knew from the beginning who they were who did not believe, and who would betray Him" (John 6:64), He had never been diffident or withdrawn from Judas; He had always treated him with the same tenderness and goodwill He had shown the others. And again, Judas was the treasurer and therefore seemed to enjoy an extra measure of trust from the others. He was probably one of the last disciples anyone would have suspected. And yet his entire association with Jesus had been nothing but a charade.

THE TRAITOR UNMASKED

In order to keep up the charade a little while longer, Judas joined the group in asking, "Rabbi, is it I?" (Matthew 26:25). The Greek expression conveys a mock incredulity. One version aptly translates it this way: "Surely it is not I, Rabbi?" (NASB).

Jesus replied simply, "You have said it" (v. 25). That remark was evidently made quietly, to Judas alone, or else the other disciples missed its significance, because the apostle John, who was reclining next to Jesus, did not pick up on it. John records that Peter signalled him to ask Jesus whom He was talking about:

Now there was leaning on Jesus' bosom one of His disciples, whom
Jesus loved. [That is John's way of signifying himself throughout
his gospel.] Simon Peter therefore motioned to him to ask who it
was of whom He spoke. Then, leaning back on Jesus' breast, he
said to Him, "Lord, who is it?" Jesus answered, "It is he to whom
I shall give a piece of bread when I have dipped it." And having
dipped the bread, He gave it to Judas Iscariot, the son of Simon.
(John 13:23–26)

Even that exchange apparently took place in whispered tones,
because none of the other disciples seemed to realize that Christ
was identifying Judas as the traitor. When He then told Judas,
"What you do, do quickly" (v. 27), John says, "No one at the table
knew for what reason He said this to him. For some thought,
because Judas had the money box, that Jesus had said to him,
'Buy those things we need for the feast,' or that he should give
something to the poor" (vv. 28–29).

John also records that after Judas took the piece of bread from
Jesus, Satan entered into him again (v. 27). As before, when Judas
arranged the betrayal with the Sanhedrin, he was possessed by
the devil. Having hardened his heart to Jesus, he became totally a
tool of the evil one.

Judas's eternal doom was now set. All that was left to be done
was the deed itself. And there was no point in dragging out the
matter. In fact, Jesus now wanted the Satan-possessed traitor out
of the room so that He could finish the Passover meal with His
true disciples. So He instructed Judas to do the deed quickly.

There is no way of knowing whether Judas's original plan was
to betray Jesus on that particular night. Of course we know from
Matthew 26:5 that the Jewish leaders would have preferred to
wait until after the feast season—still at least a week hence—to

deal with Jesus. But the divine timetable was perfect, and those events in the Upper Room sealed Judas's decision to betray Jesus that very night. He knew exactly how to do it, because Jesus' custom of praying with His disciples at Gethsemane was well established (John 18:2).

A NEW FEAST INSTITUTED

From that point on, that last Passover Seder became the institution of the New Covenant ordinance known as the Lord's Supper.

> And as they were eating, Jesus took bread, blessed and broke it, and gave it to the disciples and said, "Take, eat; this is My body." Then He took the cup, and gave thanks, and gave it to them, saying, "Drink from it, all of you. For this is My blood of the new covenant, which is shed for many for the remission of sins. But I say to you, I will not drink of this fruit of the vine from now on until that day when I drink it new with you in My Father's kingdom." And when they had sung a hymn, they went out to the Mount of Olives. (Matthew 26:26–30)

The Passover had been observed in Israel since the eve of their departure from Egypt under Moses—almost fifteen hundred years before Christ. It was the oldest of the Old Covenant rituals. It preceded the giving of the law. It was instituted before any of the other Jewish feasts. It was older than the priesthood, the tabernacle, and the rest of the Mosaic sacrificial system.

This night marked the end of all those ceremonies and the coming of the reality they foreshadowed. It was the last Passover sanctioned by God. The Old Covenant, along with all the ceremonial elements that pertained to it, was about to be brought to a close with the ushering in of a glorious New Covenant that would never pass away.

The feasts and rituals and priesthood of the Mosaic economy all pointed forward to the Great High Priest who would offer one sacrifice for sins forever. That was about to become a reality. From now on, the people of God would celebrate with a new feast that looked back on Jesus' High Priestly work in remembrance.

And so Jesus took some of the elements of the Passover meal and transformed them into the elements of the New-Covenant ordinance. It was the end of Passover for all time and the beginning of something new and greater.

Matthew states that the Passover feast was still underway. In all likelihood, they had just finished eating the lamb and were ready to move to the next phase of the Passover ritual, which would have been the passing of another cup of wine.

Jesus took some of the unleavened bread and "blessed it"— or gave thanks to God for it. Then He broke it and distributed it to the disciples saying, "Take, eat; this is My body." The saying undoubtedly jarred the disciples. It was reminiscent of Jesus' words in John 6, where He described Himself as the bread of life, the true manna that had come from heaven. In that earlier context, He was speaking to crowds of followers—many of them pseudo-disciples like Judas—and He told them, "Most assuredly, I say to you, unless you eat the flesh of the Son of Man and drink His blood, you have no life in you" (John 6:53). On that occasion His words had been so difficult to receive that "From that time many of His disciples went back and walked with Him no more" (v. 66).

There is no support here whatsoever for the superstition that gave birth to the Roman Catholic doctrine of transubstantiation—the notion that bread and wine are supernaturally transformed into the actual flesh and blood of Christ. Some insist that because Christ said, "This *is* My body," rather than "This *symbolizes* My body," He was teaching the doctrine of transubstantiation. Common sense suggests otherwise. The disciples themselves could not have understood this as anything other than symbolism. After all, His actual body had not yet been given in sacrifice. He was physically present in that body, and they had watched Him break the unleavened bread. The notion of bread actually being transubstantiated into literal flesh would have made no sense whatsoever at that moment. The plain sense of His words was quite obviously symbolic—even though the disciples undoubtedly did not yet grasp the full meaning of the symbolism.

In a similar way, Jesus had once said of John the Baptist, "This is Elijah" (Matthew 11:14, KJV)—and no one would have taken *that* statement literally either. Expressions like this are common even today, and it is a mistake to press too literal a meaning into the words. The notion of transubstantiation has been responsible for all kinds of superstition and gross idolatry, and it is important that we not misunderstand Jesus' meaning here, lest we corrupt the meaning of the ordinance.

He was instituting what would become a *remembrance* of His death (Luke 22:19), not a ritual that involves a perpetual resacrificing of His body.

After the bread was eaten, He took the cup of wine, again gave thanks, and said, "Drink from it, all of you. For this is My blood of the new covenant, which is shed for many for the remission of sins" (Matthew 26:27–28). (The Greek verb for the giving of thanks is *eucharistō,* from which we get *Eucharist,* the name often given to the observance of the Lord's Supper.)

This would have most likely been the third of four cups of wine passed during a traditional Passover Seder. The third cup was called "the cup of blessing," which is the same expression the apostle Paul uses to speak of the communion cup in 1 Corinthians 10:16.

Christ's words as He passed the cup would have stunned the disciples even more than His reference to the bread as His body. There was to the Jewish mind no more repulsive and loathsome practice than the ingestion of blood of any kind. The Old Testament ceremonial law strictly forbade the eating or drinking of any blood (Leviticus 17:14). That is why to this day kosher meats are prepared with a process designed to rid them of every trace of blood. In the early Jewish church the idea of eating blood was deemed so offensive that the Jerusalem council asked Gentile believers to abstain from the practice in deference to their Jewish brethren (Acts 15:20). Paul later made it clear that no foods were to be considered unclean if received with thanksgiving (1 Timothy 4:4). But an abhorrence of eating blood was so deeply ingrained in the Jewish consciousness that even after it was no longer deemed ceremonially unclean, many considered the practice revolting.

So for Jesus to offer the disciples a cup with the words, "Drink from it, all of you. . . . this is My blood" would surely have offended their sensibilities. It was a shocking statement, and one can easily envision the disciples exchanging startled glances and whispering among themselves about what He might possibly mean.

The fact that He called it "My blood of the new covenant" is significant. Important covenants were always ratified by the shedding of sacrificial blood. When someone entered into a covenant with his neighbor, for example, sometimes in order to solemnize the covenant a sacrificial calf would be cut in two pieces and the pieces arranged on the ground. Then the parties in the covenant would walk together between the pieces of the slaughtered animal, signifying their willingness to be cut in pieces if they violated the covenant. This kind of covenant ceremony is referred to in Jeremiah 34:18. We see it also in Genesis 15:9–18, where Jehovah put Abraham to sleep and passed between the animal parts alone, demonstrating the unconditional nature of His covenant with Abraham.

When the Mosaic covenant was instituted, Moses solemnized it by sacrificing several large oxen. He collected their blood in large basins. Then he took a branch of hyssop (a broomlike herb), dipped it into the blood, and shook it at the people, slinging sprinkles of blood over the entire congregation. On that occasion, Moses spoke words very similar to what Jesus said to the disciples in the Upper Room—"This is the blood of the covenant which the LORD has made with you" (Exodus 24:5–8).

The shedding of blood was a vital aspect of the ratification of any covenant, but in the New Covenant, the blood of Christ served a double purpose, because the theme of the New Covenant was redemption, and the shedding of blood was an essential aspect of atonement for sin. "Without shedding of blood there is no remission" (Hebrews 9:22). "For the life of the flesh is in the blood, and I have given it to you upon the altar to make atonement for your souls; for it is the blood that makes atonement for the soul" (Leviticus 17:11).

There is, unfortunately, much superstition and misunderstanding about the significance of Christ's blood. One popular book written several years ago by a well-known evangelical author suggests that there was something unique about the chemistry of Christ's blood. He surmised that Christ's blood was not human blood. Instead, he said, the blood coursing through Jesus' veins was the blood of God. Of course, that would mean that Christ's body was not fully human (an echo of the ancient Docetic heresy). Other Christians have misconstrued familiar songs about the blood of Christ (such as "There Is Power in the Blood" or "There Is a Fountain Filled with Blood"). They imagine that there is some supernatural property in Christ's blood that makes it spiritually powerful, or that Jesus' blood was supernaturally collected and preserved in a heavenly cistern like some celestial relic. A few even suppose that the literal blood of Christ is applied by some mystical means to each believer at conversion, and then collected again so that it can be perpetually applied and reapplied. And many people believe that just mentioning the blood of Christ is a powerful means of stifling demonic activity—like a Christian abracadabra. Fanciful ideas such as those spring from the same superstitious thinking that spawned the notion of transubstantiation.

When the Scriptures say we are redeemed by Christ's blood, we are not to think that His plasma or corpuscles have some supernatural property. His blood was normal human blood, just as His entire body was fully human in every aspect. The "power in the blood" that we sing about lies in the atonement He wrought by the shedding of His blood, not in the actual fluid itself.

Similarly, the scriptural references to the blood of Christ do not speak of the blood as it flowed in the veins of the living Christ; they are references to the blood atonement He offered on our behalf through His death. Apart from His dying, no amount of mere bloodshed would have had any efficacy to save sinners. So when the Bible speaks about the blood of Christ, it uses the expression as a metonymy for His atoning death.

Here at the last Passover, for example, when He passed the cup and said it symbolized the blood of the New Covenant, shed for the remission of sins, the disciples would obviously have understood this as a reference to the kind of violent death suffered by a sacrificial animal. They knew that He spoke not of bleeding per se, but a violent bloodshedding that ends in death—a sacrificial death as an atoning substitute for sinners.

Christ was already establishing in their minds the theological meaning of His death. He wanted them to understand when they saw Him bleeding and dying at the hands of Roman executioners that He was not a hapless victim of wicked men, but He was sovereignly fulfilling His role as the Lamb of God—the great Passover Lamb—who takes away sin.

And in instituting the ordinance as a remembrance of His death, He made the communion cup a perpetual reminder of this truth for all believers of all time. The point was not to impute some magical transubstantiated property to the red fluid (as Roman Catholic theology suggests), but to signify and symbolize His atoning death.

Thus as the last Passover drew to a close, a new ordinance was instituted for the church. And Jesus told the disciples that this would be the last cup He would drink with them until He drank it anew in the Father's kingdom (Matthew 26:29). By saying that, He not only underscored how imminent His departure was, but He also assured them of His return. By implication He also reassured them that they would all be together with Him in that glorious kingdom.

They could not have understood the full import of His words that evening. Only after His death and resurrection did most of these truths become clear to them. They undoubtedly sensed that something momentous was occurring, but they would have been at a loss to explain it that evening.

The meal had ended. The last Passover was complete. Matthew records that they sang a hymn—probably Psalm 118, the last hymn of the Hallel, which was the traditional way to end a Passover Seder. Either while still in the Upper Room, or shortly after leaving, Jesus prayed the lengthy prayer recorded in John 17—His high priestly prayer. And then they left for the Mount of Olives. Only Jesus fully understood the awful events that lay ahead.

ENDNOTE

1 John MacArthur, *The Legacy of Jesus* (Chicago: Moody, 1986).

3

It is written: "I will strike the Shepherd, and the sheep of the flock will be scattered."

—MATTHEW 26:31

3

 A Warning against Over-Confidence

JESUS AND HIS DISCIPLES left the Upper Room to go pray in solitude in the Garden of Gethsemane. Their route would have taken them out of the city, past the southern end of the temple mount, down into the Kidron Valley, and partway up the slope of the Mount of Olives. It was normally a half-hour's walk—no more than three-quarters of a mile. On this occasion, however, the streets and pathways would be clogged with pilgrims who had just eaten their Passover meals in borrowed rooms, as well as local citizens, most of whom would still be preparing for their Passover celebration on the following evening.

The Kidron Valley would be flowing at that time of year with runoff from seasonal rains, and the water *that* night would still be running bright crimson from the blood of a hundred thousand lambs slain just above on the temple mount a few hours before.

Gethsemane was a garden planted with olive trees. The name comes from an Aramaic word meaning "olive press," suggesting that it was a place where olives were harvested and made into oil.

In all likelihood it was a private garden owned by someone friendly to Christ who permitted Him to retreat there with His close disciples, in order to get away from the activity of city life for times of private prayer and instruction. On that site today there is still a thriving olive grove, with a few trees more than two thousand years old. Those very trees may well have been mute witnesses to the drama on that fateful evening.

The events of that final Passover evening must have seemed baffling to the disciples. Jesus was clearly troubled in His spirit by what lay ahead (cf. John 12:27; 13:21). His disciples were not accustomed to seeing Him in such a frame of mind. The Passover was a festive occasion, and yet so much of what Jesus had said to them that evening had disturbing and ominous overtones.

Either somewhere along the way, or just as they reached the garden, Jesus had still more disturbing words for the remaining disciples:

> Then Jesus said to them, "All of you will be made to stumble because of Me this night, for it is written: 'I will strike the Shepherd, and the sheep of the flock will be scattered.' But after I have been raised, I will go before you to Galilee." Peter answered and said to Him, "Even if all are made to stumble because of You, I will never be made to stumble." Jesus said to him, "Assuredly, I say to you that this night, before the rooster crows, you will deny Me three times." Peter said to Him, "Even if I have to die with You, I will not deny You!" And so said all the disciples. (Matthew 26:31–35)

Is there a true believer in Christ who has never thought about what he or she might do if confronted with the choice of denying Him or being killed? Occasionally we read about modest, everyday believers who pay the ultimate price for their faith. Recent headlines have featured several examples, such as Cassie Bernall and Rachel Scott, students at Columbine High School in Littleton, Colorado. When fellow students on a rampage held automatic weapons to their heads and asked, "Do you believe in God?" both answered yes, and both were instantly shot and killed. A host of similar violent incidents have targeted student prayer meetings. A short time before the Columbine incident, a gunman attacked a student prayer meeting in a Paducah, Kentucky, school and killed several students who had gathered around the school's flagpole for a prayer meeting.

While writing this book I was teaching in a pastors' conference in Fort Worth, Texas, on a Wednesday night. Just a few miles from the church hosting our conference was Wedgwood Baptist Church. On that same evening Wedgwood was sponsoring a student prayer meeting with hundreds of students in attendance. A fanatically anti-Christian man bent on violence walked into that prayer meeting with automatic weapons and began spraying bullets around the auditorium, killing eight people and injuring many more. In the midst of the shooting one young man, Jeremiah Neitz (who himself had been recently converted to Christ from a life of crime and street gangs), stood and challenged the gunman, telling him of his need for Christ. The gunman, apparently baffled by the youth's boldness and refusal to cower in the face of death, put his gun to his own head and committed suicide.

Most of us think from time to time about what we might do in such a situation. Few of us really expect to encounter such a severe trial, but we want to believe that we have the courage to die for Christ. And we pray that if we're ever put in such a situation, God will give us grace to be faithful.

But the sad truth is that most of us have too often denied the

Lord in less-than-life-threatening situations. We know from experience that we are woefully weak. We often remain silent when we have opportunities to speak for Christ. We tolerate unrighteousness when we ought to stand against it. We are timid when we ought to be bold. We do nothing when we ought to act. We are silent when we ought to speak out. Left to ourselves, apart from divine grace, we all lack the strength and fortitude to stand up for Christ in the face of hostility.

The disciples were no different. They *became* fearless witnesses, and ultimately all of them died for their faith or were persecuted, tortured, or exiled because of it. But they were not always so bold. And particularly on the night of Jesus' betrayal, every one of them forsook Christ and fled for their lives (Mark 14:50).

Not one of them fully realized how unprepared they were to face opposition. As they approached the place where Christ knew He would be taken captive, He began to warn the disciples that they would all stumble and deny Him that very night. Peter brashly protested that *he* would never deny Christ. He told Jesus, "Lord, I am ready to go with thee, both into prison, and to death" (Luke 22:33, KJV). He was not alone in his overconfidence. "All the disciples said the same thing too" (Matthew 26:35, NASB).

Although Christ had told them repeatedly that He would be betrayed and murdered, He had revealed to them for the first time less than two hours before that one of their own number would be the betrayer. As much as they had difficulty believing *that,* they now also responded with utter incredulity to His latest revelation—that *every one of them* would falter in the face of opposition that very night.

His words ought to have been received as a gentle exhortation to fall on their faces and plead with God for grace and strength to endure the trial. Instead, the disciples seemed to respond by trying to fortify their own self-confidence through boasting and self-determination and verbal declarations of their loyalty to Jesus. That was exactly the wrong response. They were merely bolstering a false confidence in their own strength—which was not nearly as great as they imagined.

They were about to undergo a trial that they would miserably fail. This moment would remain permanently etched in their memories as the most shameful episode of their lives. It would become a lesson about humility that none of them would ever forget. But on that night, as they approached the garden where Jesus would be betrayed and arrested, not one of them humbly heeded Christ's tender admonition. Instead, they responded with arrogant words, pounding their chests about how prepared they were to suffer for Christ's sake.

There are two powerful lessons in this account for each one of us: the utter insufficiency of our own resources and the absolute sufficiency of Christ.

THE DISCIPLES' INSUFFICIENCY

If the disciples had simply listened to Christ, they would have realized that He was gently reminding them of their insufficiency to handle such a severe trial. Rather than trying to motivate them to summon courage and self-confidence, He was reminding them of their weakness and urging them to seek *His* strength. Unfortunately, they all missed the point.

They had much yet to learn about taking up the cross and following Him. In order to do that, they needed to realize their own spiritual poverty and lean on Him for strength. His teaching had been filled with such lessons, from the beginning of His ministry. For example the very first Beatitude (and the opening sentence of the Sermon on the Mount) was, "Blessed are the poor in spirit, for theirs is the kingdom of heaven" (Matthew 5:3). He was describing a poverty of spirit that is the polar opposite of self-confidence. He held up a little child—a small toddler—and stated, "Whosoever therefore shall humble himself as this little child, the same is greatest in the kingdom of heaven" (Matthew 18:4, KJV). The child was the very picture of someone who trustingly depends on resources provided by someone else. Christ had repeatedly extolled humility and condemned the pride and self-sufficiency of the Pharisees. His teaching on the subject could not have been more clear.

Yet in the moment of their greatest trial, all the disciples could do was assert their own strength and self-sufficiency. It was a catastrophic error. "Let him who thinks he stands take heed lest he fall" (1 Corinthians 10:12).

The disciples had yet to learn the lesson of dying to themselves (1 Corinthians 15:31; 2 Corinthians 5:15; Galatians 2:20). They did not yet realize their own insufficiency for the task Jesus was calling them to (cf. 2 Corinthians 2:16). Instead of trusting in themselves, they should have been seeking strength from a higher Source (cf. 2 Corinthians 1:9; 12:9–10). They were about to learn a lesson none of them would ever forget.

Unlike Judas, the eleven remaining disciples did not deliberately and premeditatedly deny Christ. It is clear from Matthew's account that they were appalled at the very thought of such cowardice. They regarded it as one of the worst of sins to be ashamed of Christ. Christ Himself had said, "Whoever is ashamed of Me and My words in this adulterous and sinful generation, of him the Son of Man also will be ashamed when He comes in the glory of His Father with the holy angels" (Mark 8:38). He also told them, "Whosoever shall deny me before men, him will I also deny before my Father which is in heaven" (Matthew 10:33, KJV). Such an act was unthinkable to them.

But as they were soon to learn, faithfulness to Christ is impossible without total dependance on Him. The strongest disciple is utterly impotent when he trusts his own resources for courage and strength to endure. "For we do not wrestle against flesh and blood, but against principalities, against powers, against the rulers of the darkness of this age, against spiritual hosts of wickedness in the heavenly places" (Ephesians 6:12). Without spiritual armor from the Lord, we expose ourselves to the worst kinds of defeat and shame.

Peter and the others did not know it, but an unseen battle was being waged for their souls. Both John and Luke record that Jesus had given them a similar warning earlier, while they were still in the Upper Room (Luke 22:31–34; John 13:36–38). Then Jesus had told Peter, "Simon, Simon! Indeed, Satan has asked for you, that he may sift you as wheat" (Luke 22:31). The word for "you" in the Greek text is plural, indicating that this warning applied not only to Peter, but to the others as well. There, too, Peter had replied, "Lord, I am ready to go with You, both to prison and to death" (v. 33), and Jesus had already forewarned him, "I tell you, Peter, the rooster shall not crow this day before you will deny three times that you know Me" (v. 34).

Peter, wrongly assuming that the plot to take Jesus was merely a flesh-and-blood conflict, was depending on fleshly resources such as his own courage and physical stamina—and as we shall shortly see, his sword (v. 38). But such things are always insufficient weapons in a spiritual battle. "Woe to those who go down to Egypt for help, and rely on horses, who trust in chariots because they are many, and in horsemen because they are very strong, but who do not look to the Holy One of Israel, nor seek the LORD!" (Isaiah 31:1).

Now as they reached the garden, Jesus repeated His warning in more explicit terms. Once again He told Peter, "Assuredly, I say to you that this night, before the rooster crows, you will deny Me three times" (Matthew 26:34). But Peter and the disciples seemed to miss completely the seriousness of what was about to occur. Their egos were severely wounded by the suggestion that they would abandon Christ in the hour of trial. All they could do was protest about Jesus' lack of confidence in them. They were so busy asserting their own self-confidence that they were not really listening to Him. And therefore they missed the full import of what He was warning them about. There is no excuse for their being caught off guard. But they clearly had no idea of the scope of the trial they were about to undergo. Even after Jesus' repeated warnings, their sense of self-confidence was only bolstered. They remained oblivious to the Lord's tender warning. But it was a sinful, willful blindness on their part, rooted in pride and self-sufficiency. They were about to learn the dangers of pride the hard way.

CHRIST'S PERFECT SUFFICIENCY

Some might be tempted to assume that it reflects poorly on Jesus' leadership that all His followers would forsake Him at His arrest. Perhaps that is the very reason all the gospel writers included Jesus' prediction of their denial. Here again we have proof of Jesus' omniscience and His sovereign control over the events that were taking place. It was inexcusable that the disciples were caught off guard. But Jesus knew perfectly what was about to happen. His sovereignty is thus magnified by the weakness of His disciples. His faithfulness is shown in stark contrast to their unfaithfulness. His strength is made perfect in their weakness.

Christ not only knew that the disciples would abandon Him; He also knew that His prediction of their failure would go unheeded. He had already prayed for them, that their faith would not fail (Luke 22:32). And His prayer—like all His prayers—would be answered in God's perfect plan and timing. None of these events were accidental. Everything came to pass exactly as Christ foretold.

All of this underscores His absolute sovereignty. Not one event that evening came as a surprise to Him. The actions of His disciples, the actions of Judas, and the actions of the arresting soldiers were all known to Him before they occurred.

Matthew, who wrote as an eyewitness to these events, noted that Jesus Himself foretold the disciples' abandonment as a fulfillment of Old Testament prophecy. When He predicted their failure, He cited Zechariah 13:7: "Strike the Shepherd, and the sheep will be scattered." This, like so many details associated with Jesus' crucifixion, "was done that the Scriptures of the prophets might be fulfilled" (Matthew 26:56).

Within a very short time, everything Jesus had predicted would come to pass. And though the disciples would begin to feel that their entire universe was suddenly spinning out of control, Jesus kept reminding them that everything was proceeding according to God's plan.

The prophecy from Zechariah is fascinating when examined in context. Zechariah was prophesying about a time when a fountain would be opened for the spiritual cleansing of Israel. In that day, Zechariah said, false prophets would cease their wicked prophesying (Zechariah 13:2–6). A remnant of Israel would be redeemed (vv. 8–9). And in the midst of that prophecy, he included these words of verse 7: "'Awake, O sword, against My Shepherd, against the Man who is My Companion,' says the LORD

of hosts. 'Strike the Shepherd, and the sheep will be scattered.'"
The expression "My Shepherd . . . the Man who is My Companion" speaks of the Lord's anointed One, the Messiah. The Hebrew word for "My companion" can also mean "My equal"—signifying Christ's deity. But the most remarkable thing about Zechariah's prophecy is that it is Jehovah Himself who calls for the Shepherd to be stricken with the sword.

So the Zechariah prophecy is more evidence from the Old Testament that the crucifixion of Christ was God's plan. He was still in control, even when it seemed from the human perspective that Satan and the forces of evil were getting the upper hand.

Notice Jesus' next words to the disciples. Immediately after citing the prophecy about scattering the sheep, He added, "But after I have been raised, I will go before you to Galilee" (Matthew 26:32). He had given similar words of reassurance in the Upper Room when He told Peter Satan had desired to sift them as wheat: "I have prayed for thee, that thy faith fail not: and when thou art converted, strengthen thy brethren" (Luke 22:32, KJV). Thus He reassured them that even though it would seem that night as if their world were coming to an end, they all had a future ministry to prepare for. Christ still had power over death—even in the midst of His own murder.

Of course, the words of encouragement were lost on the disciples at that moment, but later they would remember what He had said and their faith would be strengthened. They had seen Him raise the dead on several occasions before this. They were present at the raising of Lazarus, when He told Martha, "I am the resurrection and the life" (John 11:25). All of these things would eventually fall into place in their thinking, but for now they were too bewildered and troubled to make sense of what He meant. Their minds were no doubt still reeling from the stinging blow to their pride because of His prediction that they would fail Him. They were too busy trying to prop up their own self-confidence to have much faith in Him at the moment.

Had they seen beyond their own fear and confusion, they would have known that Christ was the same sovereign Lord they had always known. He was as much in control now as when He fed the multitudes, healed the sick, and raised the dead. They should have been looking to Him as the all-sufficient One who would see them through this trial. In fact, Christ's omniscience should have been a reminder and a proof to them of His absolute sufficiency. But instead, they had in a sense forsaken Him already in their hearts, by looking too much to their own abilities to see them through the trial that was ahead.

Christ's gracious promises to them about their future ministry reveal His love and grace for these men, even before they failed. As He promised, He did go before them to Galilee. That same promise was reaffirmed to them immediately after Jesus' resurrection, by the angel who met Mary Magdalene and the other Mary at the opened tomb. The angel told the women, "Go quickly and tell His disciples that He is risen from the dead, and indeed He is going before you into Galilee; there you will see Him" (Matthew 28:7). Christ Himself appeared to the two women a few moments later, and He reiterated the instructions: "Do not be afraid. Go and tell My brethren to go to Galilee, and there they will see Me" (v. 10).

It was there in Galilee that Jesus appeared to Peter and forgave him for his unfaithfulness. Peter, along with James, John, and several other disciples, had returned to fishing. Having fished all night, they caught nothing. At daybreak, they saw a man on the shore, who told them, "Cast the net on the right side of the boat, and you will find some" (John 21:6). They did as He said and caught so many fish in their nets that they could not haul the nets in. This was exactly what had happened when Peter first met Christ and was called to discipleship (Luke 5:4–11). So Peter immediately recognized that it was Jesus on the shore. He dived out of the boat and swam to Him. Jesus was preparing breakfast for the disciples as a token of His love for them.

After breakfast that morning, Christ asked Peter, "Simon, son of Jonah, do you love Me more than these?" Peter replied, "Yes, Lord; You know that I love You" (John 21:15). The response was timid, uncertain. Peter used a different word for "love" than Jesus had employed. Peter chose a word that speaks of brotherly affection. And he neglected to respond to the most important part of Jesus' question; he said nothing about whether his love for Christ was greater than all else.

Peter's love for Christ had certainly not diminished. But now he was guarding against his well-known propensity for speaking brashly. In the garden, he had boasted of his willingness to die for Christ, and then he had immediately failed. Now he was being guarded and cautious in the claims he made. He had denied Christ three times, so Christ gave him three opportunities to express his love. But John reports that "Peter was grieved because He said to him the third time, 'Do you love Me?' And he said to Him, 'Lord, You know all things; You know that I love You'" (v. 17).

Notice that Peter appealed to Christ's omniscience. Still smarting from his own failure, Peter was keenly aware that Christ had foreseen it. Jesus had looked into his heart and knew it better than Peter himself did (cf. Jeremiah 17:9). He now realized that Christ knew precisely the level of his commitment, so boasting about how much he loved Him was pointless. Besides, in the wake of his own failure, Peter's cocky self-assurance was shattered. He probably doubted his own ability to assess his love for Christ correctly. And so he appealed to Christ's omniscience, which had proved infallible throughout the whole drama.

Peter had learned a great lesson. He was beginning to trust Christ's sufficiency rather than his own. He was looking to Christ to assess his heart rather than thinking he knew it all. His failure had punctured his pride, and now we see nothing of the swaggering self-assurance Peter had shown on the way to Gethsemane.

Fewer than forty days later, at Pentecost, Peter stood boldly before crowds of people—many of them the same ones who had crucified Jesus. This time Peter proclaimed the gospel with a new kind of boldness. It was not the foolhardy brashness of fleshly overconfidence, but the holy boldness that comes from being under the control of the Holy Spirit.

In fact, after Pentecost all eleven disciples were markedly changed men. These same men who deserted their Master out of craven fear became intrepid witnesses for Him. When they were told to stop preaching by the high priest (the same high priest who had them cowering in fear on the eve of Jesus' crucifixion) their response was to keep right on preaching. They told the high priest, "We ought to obey God rather than men" (Acts 5:29). Though beaten, imprisoned, and threatened with death, they kept right on preaching. In fact, when an angel supernaturally released them from prison, rather than going into hiding, they went straight back to the temple and began preaching publicly again, right under the high priest's nose (Acts 5:18–21). Were these the same men who forsook Jesus and fled in the hour of His betrayal?

They were the same men, but now they were filled with the Holy Spirit. They were drawing on a power that was not their own. They had set aside their reckless self-assurance and were depending on the sufficiency of their Lord. That made all the difference in the world. Clearly they had all learned a great lesson from their failure. These same men who all forsook Jesus and fled on the night of His arrest spent the rest of their lives standing up for Him, in the face of every imaginable threat and persecution. They never abandoned their Lord again.

Here is the greatest proof of the sufficiency of Christ: He graciously restored and empowered these men to serve Him, even in the wake of the most catastrophic kind of spiritual collapse. His all-sufficient grace redeemed them from their worst failure. Christ Himself drew them back, forgave them, commissioned them for service, and empowered them to succeed where they once had failed so miserably.

4

"O My Father, if this cup cannot pass away from Me unless I drink it, Your will be done."

—MATTHEW 26:42

4

 The Agony in the Garden

WHEN JESUS ENTERED GETHSEMANE, He knew He would be arrested there and taken through a series of trials and humiliations that would carry Him relentlessly to the cross. In fact, when the apostle John describes the arrival of the soldiers for Jesus' arrest, he records this fact: "Jesus therefore, *knowing all things that would come upon Him,* went forward and said to them, 'Whom are you seeking?'" (John 18:4, emphasis added).

Again and again we see that all the Gospel writers deliberately stress Jesus' sovereign omniscience throughout the crucifixion narratives. Their focus never strays far from the fact of His absolute foreknowledge and control of everything that was occurring around Him. All the gospel writers made it clear that Jesus "[knew] all things that would come upon Him." Nothing that night was accidental. Nothing took Him by surprise. He was fully aware of everything that was happening. Nothing was out of His and the Father's control.

This also means that Jesus understood fully all that His dying would entail. He knew in advance about all the pain and agony and taunting and humiliation He would have to bear. Before He ever set foot in that garden, He knew the awful truth about what He would have to endure. But He was nonetheless prepared to submit Himself completely and unreservedly to the Father's will, in order to accomplish the eternal plan of redemption.

In His prayer that night He grappled with these very issues in the most candid terms. It is one of the most astonishing and mysterious passages in all of Scripture. It reveals His own striving with the terrifying reality of what He was about to endure. Here we have an amazing window into the heart of the God-man.

By the time Jesus reached Gethsemane with His disciples, it would have been nearing midnight. All of them were showing signs of fatigue at this late hour. It was the end of a hectic week and the close of a busy day. But Christ had business in the garden that was more important than sleep, and nothing would deter Him from going there to pray.

Christ was fully human in every sense. He was beset with the same physical limitations that are common to humanity. He, too, felt fatigue (John 4:6; Mark 4:38). He knew what it was to be hungry (Matthew 21:18). He could be stricken with thirst like any normal person (John 4:7; 19:28). He also experienced the full range of human emotions. At times we see Him weeping and mourning (John 11:35; Luke 19:41). On a few occasions, He showed anger (John 2:15–17). Scripture never explicitly records that He laughed or smiled, but it would clearly be a mistake to conclude that He went through life with a gloomy countenance. We know He rejoiced, particularly when sinners were converted (Luke 15:4–32). His reputation among the Pharisees certainly suggests that He was no dour recluse, but a joyful and gregarious "friend of tax collectors and sinners" (Luke 7:34).

He was fully human like us in every regard, except for our

sinfulness. If Scripture seems to stress His sorrow and grief more than His joy, it is only because it is such a great comfort to us in our times of grief to know that He has fully experienced the depth of human sorrow—and to a degree that we cannot imagine. During His prayer that night in the garden, every sorrow He had ever known seemed to assault Him at once. That, combined with an obvious sense of dread for the ordeal He faced on the following day, gives us a remarkable insight into "the Man Christ Jesus" and His mediatorial work on our behalf.

Jeremiah wrote the Book of Lamentations as a dirge for the miseries of Jerusalem under the Lord's hand of affliction. But certainly Lamentations 1:12 is apropos to describe the sorrows of Christ under the afflicting hand of His Father: "Is it nothing to you, all ye that pass by? Behold, and see if there be any sorrow like unto my sorrow, which is done unto me, wherewith the LORD hath afflicted me in the day of his fierce anger" (KJV).

Never was so much sorrow emanating from the soul of one individual. We could never comprehend the depth of Christ's agony because, frankly, we cannot perceive the wickedness of sin as He could. Nor can we appreciate the terrors of divine wrath the way He did. The sorrow He expresses in the Gethsemane prayer is therefore beyond our comprehension. We should not wonder if the full meaning of the prayer seems to elude us. And yet there is also a wealth of clear insight in this passage that is often missed.

Here is Matthew's account of what happened:

Then Jesus came with them to a place called Gethsemane, and said to the disciples, "Sit here while I go and pray over there." And He took with Him Peter and the two sons of Zebedee, and He began to be sorrowful and deeply distressed. Then He said to them, "My soul is exceedingly sorrowful, even to death. Stay here and watch with Me." He went a little farther and fell on His face, and prayed, saying, "O My Father, if it is possible, let this cup pass from Me; nevertheless, not as I will, but as You will." Then He came to the disciples and found them asleep, and said to Peter, "What? Could you not watch with Me one hour? Watch and pray, lest you enter into temptation. The spirit indeed is willing, but the flesh is weak." Again, a second time, He went away and prayed, saying, "O My Father, if this cup cannot pass away from Me unless I drink it, Your will be done." And He came and found them asleep again, for their eyes were heavy. So He left them, went away again, and prayed the third time, saying the same words. (Matthew 26:36–44)

Three aspects of Christ's incomprehensible struggle are high-lighted in that passage: His sorrow, His supplication, and His submission.

HIS SORROW

Gethsemane was a familiar place to the disciples. Even Judas knew where Jesus would be that night, according to the apostle John, because "Jesus often met there with His disciples" (John 18:2). Most likely this was a walled olive grove. It seems to have had a single entrance, and Jesus left most of the disciples at the entrance, while He went inside to pray with Peter, James, and John. These three disciples constituted an inner circle among the disciples. Jesus often allowed the three of them to accompany Him on special occasions when the other disciples were not permitted to follow (cf. Mark 5:37; Matthew 17:1).

Why did He bring these three? Primarily for *their* benefit. They were privileged to be witnesses to Christ's struggle in the darkest hour of His trial. From His example, they would learn a great lesson in how to handle affliction. And even though they kept falling asleep, they witnessed enough to see how Jesus prayed to get a sense of the incredible depth of agony He was suffering.

The disciples left at the entrance of the garden may have been accustomed to watching the gate, lest anyone disturb the Lord while He was in prayer. On this particular night, they should also have been engaged in prayer for themselves. After all, Jesus had just told them of the awful trial they were about to undergo. They could see that He was troubled. He had done everything He could to alert them to the danger that was at hand. According to Luke, Jesus instructed them all, "Pray that you may not enter into temptation" (Luke 22:40). Matthew records that He awoke Peter, James, and John after they fell asleep the first and second times, and He repeated the admonition each time. Yet there is no suggestion that any of the disciples ever uttered a single word of prayer. This shows how smug they were in their self-confidence. Nothing suggests that they offered Christ any personal support or encouragement. In fact, there's a profound irony in the fact that the sinless, omnipotent Son of God felt such a great need for prayer that evening, and yet His weak, vulnerable disciples apparently had no sense of the desperate need of the hour. They were deaf to what He had told them.

This is typical of the sinful heart. In our fleshly and fallen state we are often oblivious to our own spiritual poverty and weakness. Yet even in His sinlessness, Christ was keenly aware of the weakness of human flesh, and He could not sleep when the need for communion with God was so urgent. The disciples, on the other hand, all fell asleep at their posts.

How could they fall asleep? Perhaps they were feeling safe in a familiar environment. In all probability, no one else ever came to this place at night. Forgetting that one of their own number would be the betrayer, they imagined that they were safe. They succumbed to the fatigue they were all feeling. Luke also says their deep sorrow also contributed to their sleepiness (Luke 22:45). Depression and confusion often make us want to sleep. Their troubled minds were seeking an escape. And so they fell asleep, leaving Jesus to bear His anguish all alone.

It was no hyperbole when Jesus told the disciples that His distress was so severe that it had brought Him to the very brink of death. The agony He bore in the garden was literally sufficient to kill Him—and may well have done so if God were not preserving Him for another means of death. Luke records that "His sweat became like great drops of blood falling down to the ground" (Luke 22:44). That describes a rare but well-documented malady known as *hematidrosis* that sometimes occurs under heavy emotional distress. Subcutaneous capillaries burst under stress and the blood mingles with one's perspiration, exiting through the sweat glands.

Why was He feeling such agony? It might seem natural to assume He was dreading the physical pain of the cross and the tortures He would suffer on the way to Calvary. But many have suffered crucifixion without sweating blood at the thought of it. It is inconceivable to think that the Son of God would be suffering such measureless agony for fear of what men could do to Him. He Himself had taught: "Do not fear those who kill the body but cannot kill the soul" (Matthew 10:28).

It certainly was not death per se that troubled His soul so violently. After all, He had come to die. This was the hour for which He had come. It is inconceivable that He would have second thoughts about dying at this late stage. John 12:27 records an earlier prayer of Jesus, spoken in public, in which he said, "Now My soul is troubled, and what shall I say? 'Father, save Me from this hour'? But for this purpose I came to this hour."

Here in the garden, however, He prays, "O My Father, if it is possible, let this cup pass from Me." Is He having second thoughts about dying? Is He praying to be delivered from the cross? Some commentators who want to avoid that conclusion have suggested that the "cup" He prays to be delivered from is the threat of a premature death in the garden. According to their interpretation, He was praying that the plan of redemption might not be derailed by His dying before He reached the cross.

However, that ignores the biblical significance of the term "cup." The apostle John recounts how shortly after this, when Jesus is being arrested and Peter tries to use his sword to stop the arrest, "Jesus said to Peter, 'Put your sword into the sheath. Shall I not drink the cup which My Father has given Me?'" (John 18:11). So it is evident that the Father *did* give Christ the cup to drink after all.

What is the cup? It is not merely death. It is not the physical pain of the cross. It was not the scourging or the humiliation. It was not the horrible thirst, the torture of having nails driven through His body, or the disgrace of being spat upon or beaten. It was not even all those things combined. All of those were the very things Christ Himself had said *not* to fear. He said, "And I say to you, My friends, do not be afraid of those who kill the body, and after that have no more that they can do" (Luke 12:4).

"But," He went on to add, "I will show you whom you should fear: Fear Him who, after He has killed, has power to cast into hell; yes, I say to you, fear Him!" (v. 5). Clearly, what Christ dreaded most about the cross—the cup from which He asks to be delivered if possible—was the outpouring of divine wrath He would have to endure from His holy Father.

The *cup* was a well-known Old Testament symbol of divine wrath against sin. Isaiah 51:17 says, "Awake, awake! Stand up, O

Jerusalem, You who have drunk at the hand of the LORD the cup of His fury; you have drunk the dregs of the cup of trembling, and drained it out." In Jeremiah 25:15–16, the Lord tells the prophet, "'Take this wine cup of fury from My hand, and cause all the nations, to whom I send you, to drink it. And they will drink and stagger and go mad because of the sword that I will send among them.'" He adds this instruction: "'Therefore you shall say to them, "Thus says the LORD of hosts, the God of Israel: 'Drink, be drunk, and vomit! Fall and rise no more, because of the sword which I will send among you.'" And it shall be, if they refuse to take the cup from your hand to drink, then you shall say to them, "Thus says the LORD of hosts: 'You shall certainly drink!'"" (vv. 27–28).

There the cup symbolizes a judgment that God forces the wicked to drink. They drink until they become drunk, and physically ill, and they vomit. It is as if God says to the sinner, "You like sin? Fine. Drink your fill." And He makes them keep drinking of the consequences of their own sin, so that the very thing they sought after becomes the judgment He force-feeds them; the thing they loved becomes something that makes them sick and ultimately destroys them. Similar imagery using a cup to symbolize divine judgment is found throughout the Old Testament (cf. Lamentations 4:21–22; Ezekiel 23:31–34; and Habakkuk 2:16).

So when Christ prayed that if possible the cup might pass from Him, He spoke of drinking the cup of divine judgment. Do not imagine for a moment that Christ feared the earthly pain of crucifixion. He would not have trembled at the prospect of what men could do to Him. There was not one ounce of the fear of man in Him. But the next day He would "bear the sins of many" (Hebrews 9:28)—and the fullness of divine wrath would fall on Him. In some mysterious way that our human minds could never fathom, God the Father would turn His face from Christ the Son, and Christ would bear the full brunt of the divine fury against sin.

Remember, Isaiah 53:10 says, "It pleased the LORD to bruise Him; He has put Him to grief." When Christ hung on the cross, He was bearing the sins of His people and He was suffering the wrath of God on their behalf. Second Corinthians 5:21 explains the cross in a similar way: "He made Him who knew no sin to be sin for us." In other words, on the cross, God imputed our sin to Christ and then punished Him for it (cf. 1 Peter 2:24).

The price of the sin that Christ bore was the full fury of divine wrath, and He paid it in full. That explains His cry of anguish in Matthew 27:46: "My God, My God, why have You forsaken Me?" That cry from the cross reflected the extreme bitterness of the cup He was given. No wonder He sought to have the cup pass from Him.

Didn't He realize that there was no way the cup could pass from him? *Of course He did.* So why did He pray like this in the garden? Because this was an honest expression of the dread He was feeling at the moment. He was not actually hoping to be released from the role of sin-bearer. And that is made clear by the remainder of His prayer: "Nevertheless, not as I will, but as You will" (Matthew 26:39). Notice that the second time He prayed, "O My Father, if this cup cannot pass away from Me unless I drink it, Your will be done." As the intensity of the agony increases, so does the sense of His determination to do the will of His Father.

Christ's prayer is simply an honest expression of human passion. And what is revealed in the prayer is the systematic surrender of those human passions to the divine will.

When Christ took on human flesh, he also took on Himself all the natural weaknesses of humanity—except for those that are inherently sinful. Hebrews 4:15 says, "We do not have a High Priest who cannot sympathize with our weaknesses, but was in all points tempted as we are, yet without sin." As we noted at the outset of this chapter, Christ experienced every infirmity of human nature except for sin. He grew weary; He felt hunger; He suffered pain. And here in the garden, He experienced the deepest kind of sorrow, and dread, and troubling of His soul—even to the point of death. His prayer simply is an outpouring of those very human feelings. It shows us the humanity of Christ as clearly as anything in Scripture.

What motivates Christ's praying here is not a *sinful* weakness, but normal human infirmity—no different from his hunger, thirst, or fatigue. Christ certainly had no masochistic love of suffering. There would be something inhuman about Him if He did not look forward to the cross with a deep uneasiness and dread of what was to come. But this is not a craven fear; it is the same horror and foreboding any of us would feel if we knew we were about to undergo something extremely painful. In Jesus' case, however, the agony is infinitely magnified, because of the nature of what He faced.

Nowhere does the Bible ever declare that Jesus' deity makes Him something *more* than a man, or something *other* than human. Scripture never allows the divine nature of Christ to overshadow or diminish His human nature. On the contrary, everything Scripture says about Christ's role as our Savior depends on the fact that He is fully and completely a man. Hebrews 2:17 underscores the point: "*In all things He had to be made like His brethren,* that He might be a merciful and faithful High Priest in things pertaining to God, to make propitiation for the sins of the people" (emphasis added).

Our Lord was not merely playing at being human. He was human in the fullest sense. He took on *all* our infirmities except for our sin. And at this moment in the garden, His humanity manifested itself as clearly as at any time ever in His ministry. We can certainly understand His emotions: horror at the prospect of what God wanted Him to do; consternation over the reality of what that would cost Him; and a very real desire to avoid God's wrath if there was any possible way. All of that contributed to the overwhelming sense of sorrow He was feeling as He anticipated the cross.

In short, Jesus was grieved because He knew that all the guilt of all the sin of all the redeemed of all time would be imputed to Him, and He would bear the full brunt of divine wrath on behalf of others. The holy Son of God who had never known even the most insignificant sin would *become* sin—an object of God's fury (2 Corinthians 5:21). The thought of it literally made Him sweat blood.

HIS SUPPLICATION

So Christ's sense of dread and foreboding as He faced the cross was a natural expression of human emotion. His desire to escape the wrath of God was a normal, and perfectly understandable, human feeling. But that desire, and all His human emotions, had to be consciously, deliberately surrendered to the will of God. The feelings themselves were not sinful. What is sinful is pursuing human feelings and preferences at the expense of God's will. Jesus knew that, and His entire life was therefore characterized by a constant, systematic, premeditated, voluntary submission to His Father's will. He said, "I always do those things that please Him" (John 8:29); "My food is to do the will of Him who sent Me, and to finish His work" (4:34); "I can of Myself do nothing. As I hear, I judge; and My judgment is righteous, because I do not seek My own will but the will of the Father who sent Me" (5:30); "For I have come down from heaven, not to do My own will, but the will of Him who sent Me" (6:38).

The words of His prayer in the garden simply reflect how that submission occurred. The prayer is an honest expression of the human feelings of Christ. He sincerely dreaded the prospect of the Father's wrath, and He wished to avoid it if there had been any possible way.

But why is He praying this prayer at this hour? After all, He had covenanted with God in eternity past to die as an atoning sacrifice for sin. Surely He always knew the cup of God's wrath was an unavoidable aspect of that atoning work.

All of that is true, but in His humanity, Christ had to be feeling the burden in a way He had never felt it before. The man Christ Jesus was approaching His hour. All His normal human feelings would have intensified as the hour approached. The full weight of sorrow and dread was welling up in Him as He stood on the threshold of taking up His cross. The prayer is an outpouring of those passions. It is proof that He was, after all, fully human in every sense.

His prayer in the garden served another divinely ordained purpose. It was an example to Peter and the other apostles. Of course Christ already knew that there was no possible way to avoid the outpouring of God's wrath. Surely there was no real question in His mind about whether these things were avoidable. And yet He prayed this prayer aloud for a purpose.

Jesus frequently prayed aloud for the sake of others who were listening (cf. John 11:42). There is every reason to think that this prayer in the garden was prayed aloud partly for the sake of the apostles who were listening nearby. When Jesus brought Peter, James, and John with Him into the garden, He asked them to wait nearby and watch with Him. Knowing that Satan was preparing to sift them like wheat, Jesus' prayer was a model for them. They could have learned a lot from listening to Him pray.

Perhaps that is why His pleas to the Father are interspersed with entreaties for the disciples to stay awake. Notice His words in verse Matthew 26:41: "Watch and pray, lest you enter into temptation. The spirit indeed is willing, but the flesh is weak." At that very moment, Jesus Himself was battling the infirmities of His own humanity. Again, these were not sinful infirmities, but normal human passions, appetites, and feelings which, if not subjugated to the divine will, can lead to sin.

Peter sinned because he slept. It's normally no sin to sleep, but at that moment, Christ had given him work to do. He was supposed to be awake and watching and praying with Christ. Peter's fatigue, combined with his great sorrow that evening, made him seek refuge in sleep. Fatigue and sorrow were not sinful in themselves, but those things needed to be submitted to the will of God. Peter's *spirit* was certainly willing (v. 33). But his flesh was weak. He should have been praying the way Christ was— consciously submitting his will to the Father's will, and looking to God for the strength to endure.

The words of Christ's prayer reveal a touching intimacy between Father and Son. Whenever He prayed, Christ always addressed God as "Father." (The one exception was as He hung on the cross, feeling the weight of divine wrath, and He prayed in Aramaic the words of Psalm 22:1, "'Eloi, Eloi, lama sabachthani?' which is translated, 'My God, My God, why have You forsaken Me?'"—Mark 15:34.) As far as the Jewish leaders were concerned, praying to God as "Father" was an unorthodox way to address God, because they felt it showed too much familiarity or intimacy. In fact, they sought to kill Jesus on more than one occasion because He constantly called God His Father—and they correctly understood His claim to sonship as a claim of absolute equality with God (John 5:18; cf. 10:30–33). Jesus' unique and eternal Sonship does establish His eternal equality with God (Hebrews 1:4–8). He is God's only begotten Son. But all Christians also have a special status of sonship accorded by their adoption (Galatians 4:4–5). And therefore Christ taught even His disciples to address God in prayer as "Father."

Here in the garden, however, we encounter the only place in all of Scripture where Christ addressed God in prayer as "*My Father*" (Matthew 26:39, 42), intensifying the intimacy of the expression. In fact, Mark records that He prayed, "Abba, Father, all things are possible for You. Take this cup away from Me; nevertheless, not what I will, but what You will" (Mark 14:36). "Abba" is the Aramaic equivalent of "Daddy," or "Papa"—a still more intimate, even childlike, expression of trust and affection.

Christ's prayer was above all a prayer of submission. The real gist of the prayer, the petition that dominated Christ's plea, is not the request to let the cup pass, but the still higher purpose reflected in His repeated request, "Your will be done" (Matthew 26:42). Each wave of His praying stressed the same thing: "My Father, if it is possible, let this cup pass from Me; nevertheless, *not as I will, but as You will*" (v. 39). "O My Father, if this cup cannot pass away from Me unless I drink it, *Your will be done*" (v. 42). "He left them, went away again, and prayed the third time, *saying the same words*" (v. 44; emphasis added in all preceding quotations).

His natural human desire was to avoid if possible the awful judgment He was about to suffer. But His overriding desire—the ultimate answer to prayer He was pleading for—was that God's will be done.

HIS SUBMISSION

When Christ prays, "not as I will, but as You will," we are not to think that there is any disparity between the will of the Father and the will of the Son. Instead, what we see here is the Son consciously, deliberately, voluntarily subjugating all His natural human feelings to the perfect will of the Father. The prayer is the consummate example of how Christ in His humanity *always* surrendered His will to the will of the Father in all things—precisely so that there would be no conflict between the divine will and His human feelings.

There's a poignant lesson here. Remember that Christ had no sinful appetites, no desires that were perverted by sin, no inclination ever to do wrong. Yet if He needed to submit His appetites and passions to the will of God with such deliberate, purposeful dedication, how much more do *we* need to be deliberate in surrendering our hearts, our souls, our minds, and our strength to God? All our infirmities, our desires, our appetites, and our very wills—must be consciously submitted to the will of God if we expect to be able to live our lives to the glory of God.

Christ's prayer was not for the cup to pass *at any cost*. He asked to be relieved of the cup only if there were some other way to accomplish the plan of God. God's response to this prayer proves definitively that there was no possible way to achieve the redemption of sinners short of the sacrifice of His own Son. God did not send Christ to die frivolously. If there had been another way, He would have done it. But there was no other way, and that is why the cup did not pass from Christ.

It is certain that Christ knew this when He prayed the prayer. This whole question was worked out in the eternal counsel of God, before the foundation of the world, long before Christ ever came to earth. He knew that if He was going to be the Lamb of God to take away the sins of the world, then that meant He must endure the wrath of God in the process.

That suggests yet another reason why Christ prayed this prayer. Not only was it a true expression of His human passions, expressing His very real dread and horror at the thought of what the cross would mean for Him; not only was it an important example for Peter and the other disciples (as well as all Christians for all time); but it also unfolds the mystery of what took place in eternity past between the members of the Godhead. As God the Father and God the Son covenanted together with the Holy Spirit to redeem the elect, it was agreed that Christ would become a man and die to pay the atoning price.

The apostle Paul spoke of this in his epistle to Titus. He opens with these words: "Paul, a bondservant of God and an apostle of Jesus Christ, according to the faith of God's elect and the acknowledgment of the truth which accords with godliness, in hope of eternal life which God, who cannot lie, *promised before time began*" (Titus 1:1–2, emphasis added). If God promised eternal life before time began—before there were any creatures to make such a promise to—to whom did He promise it? It is clear that this describes a covenant that took place between the Members of the Godhead for the redemption of the elect.

Second Timothy 1:9 contains an echo of Titus 1:2. There the apostle Paul says God "saved us and called us with a holy calling, not according to our works, but according to His own purpose and grace *which was given to us in Christ Jesus before time began*" (emphasis added). In other words, the eternal guarantee of our salvation involved a promise made by the Father to the Son before time began. Our entire hope of eternal life consists in that eternal promise made to Christ.

Because of His eternal love for His Son, God the Father promised Him a redeemed people. That is why Christ often spoke of the redeemed as those whom the Father had given to Him (John 17:9, 11, 24; cf. 6:37–39).

For His part, Christ covenanted to die for their redemption. Mere animal sacrifices could not atone for sin. There was only one means by which they could be redeemed. A human Substitute, so perfectly righteous that no fault could ever be found in Him, would have to bear the penalty for sin as their Substitute. And only the incarnate Son of God was good enough. Therefore, as His part in the covenant for our redemption, Christ agreed to come to earth for the express purpose of dying as a sacrifice for sin. He lovingly submitted Himself to the Father's will in order to purchase redemption for His people. That is the whole point of Hebrews 10:4–9:

It is not possible that the blood of bulls and goats could take away sins. Therefore, when He came into the world, He said: "Sacrifice and offering You did not desire, but a body You have prepared for Me. In burnt offerings and sacrifices for sin You had no pleasure. Then I said, 'Behold, I have come; in the volume of the book it is written of Me; to do Your will, O God.'" Previously saying, "Sacrifice and offering, burnt offerings, and offerings for sin You did not desire, nor had pleasure in them" (which are offered according to the law), then He said, "Behold, I have come to do Your will, O God."

So Christ's submission to the Father's will was an expression of His eternal love for the Father. As abhorrent and mysterious as it is to think of the Son's dying and the Father's pouring out His wrath on the Son—the underlying purpose of redemption was a pure expression of love between Father and Son. And thus in eternity past the Son willingly, deliberately submitted Himself to the Father's will, and the path to the cross was set.

That is the main truth unfolded for us in Jesus' prayer in the garden. Here we see in microcosm the whole process described in Philippians 2:6–8, where Christ, "did not consider equality with God something to be grasped, but made himself nothing, taking the very nature of a servant, being made in human likeness. And being found in appearance as a man, he humbled himself and became obedient to death—even death on a cross!" (NIV). His Gethsemane prayer gives us a window into His soul and heart as He made that surrender, and it reveals what a supreme sacrifice it was for Him to die on our behalf.

When Christ finished praying, He had the victory He sought. He emerged from His agony in perfect harmony with the will of His Father. He was prepared to face the cross and drink to the dregs the bitter cup of the Father's wrath against sin.

His enemies were already approaching. The calmness with which Christ would meet them—and the quiet grace He would show throughout His whole ordeal—are graphic proof that God the Father heard and answered His Son's heart's cry in Gethsemane.

5

"Judas, are you betraying the Son of Man with a kiss?"

—LUKE 22:48

5

 The Kiss of the Traitor

FROM A HUMAN VANTAGE POINT, the remaining events of that tragic night would seem to bring nothing but disgrace and defeat for the Son of God. A human observer might think that Jesus' prayer in the garden went unheeded by His Father, and that everything from that point on suddenly spun out of control for Jesus. That was undoubtedly what the disciples thought.

They had never been in a situation like this before. Many times Jesus had been challenged by hostile Pharisees and Sadducees, but always He had confounded and silenced them. On numerous occasions, His enemies had sought to take Him by force or threatened Him with bodily harm. But He had always eluded their grasp, sometimes by miraculous means. They were accustomed to seeing Him in the victor's role; never had He been in the role of a victim.

Suddenly everything began to go wrong—or so it seemed. An armed mob arrived on the scene to arrest Him. Judas quite unexpectedly betrayed Him in the most despicable manner with a hypocritical kiss. When Peter tried to intervene with force, Jesus stopped him with a stern rebuke. Finally, the disciples, gripped with fear, abandoned their Master and fled. Each turn of events seemed to bring more disgrace and defeat upon Jesus. That is surely how it seemed to all the observers on the scene that night.

And yet the one overarching reality that arises out of all the biblical accounts of this episode is the tranquil majesty of Christ, whose absolute sovereignty and calm, triumphant demeanor remained uncompromised throughout the whole ordeal. It is a remarkable scene, and Matthew describes it in graphic terms:

Then He came to His disciples and said to them, "Are you still sleeping and resting? Behold, the hour is at hand, and the Son of Man is being betrayed into the hands of sinners. Rise, let us be going. See, My betrayer is at hand."

And while He was still speaking, behold, Judas, one of the twelve, with a great multitude with swords and clubs, came from the chief priests and elders of the people. Now His betrayer had given them a sign, saying, "Whomever I kiss, He is the One; seize Him." Immediately he went up to Jesus and said, "Greetings, Rabbi!" and kissed Him. But Jesus said to him, "Friend, why have you come?" Then they came and laid hands on Jesus and took Him. And suddenly, one of those who were with Jesus stretched out his hand and drew his sword, struck the servant of the high priest, and cut off his ear. But Jesus said to him, "Put your sword in its place, for all who take the sword will perish by the sword. Or do you think that I cannot now pray to My Father, and He will provide Me with more than twelve legions of angels? How then could the Scriptures be fulfilled, that it must happen thus?" In that hour Jesus said to the multitudes, "Have you come out, as against a robber, with swords and clubs to take Me? I sat daily with you, teaching in the temple, and you did not seize Me. But all this was done that the Scriptures of the prophets might be fulfilled." Then all the disciples forsook Him and fled. (Matthew 26:45–56)

Jesus had repeatedly urged the disciples to stay awake and pray with Him. Three times He had prayed, and after each prayer He had awakened them and exhorted them to pray too. Christ's struggle in the garden represented an intense spiritual conflict with the powers of darkness. Earlier, in the Upper Room, He had told the disciples, "I will no longer talk much with you, for the ruler of this world is coming, and he has nothing in Me" (John 14:30). Satan had tempted Christ at the beginning of His ministry, and Christ had withstood every one of his ploys (Matthew 4:1–11)—and never let up all through His life. But the agony in the garden represents a final, desperate frontal assault from the evil one, and Christ had again emerged victorious. There was absolutely nothing in Him that Satan could take advantage of.

A MOB APPROACHES

But Satan was already mounting a different kind of attack. Judas was approaching with a large armed mob sent by the chief priests and elders from the temple.

Notice that Matthew still refers to Judas as "one of the twelve" (Matthew 26:47). He is often designated that way in the New Testament. In fact, all four gospels use the expression to describe Judas (cf. Mark 14:10, 43; Luke 22:47; John 6:71), while only once is another disciple (Thomas) described as "one of the twelve" (John 20:24). The gospel writers deliberately stressed Judas's status as one of the twelve in order to accent the sense of shock and betrayal they all felt when he turned out to be a traitor.

By way of contrast, apocryphal accounts of Judas often portrayed him as overtly diabolical. Some early writers invented fanciful tales about him to make him seem as conspicuously perverse and grotesquely evil as possible. But the truth is that Judas seemed like a typical disciple. He had obviously never given the other disciples any reason to distrust him, because they were all caught completely off guard when he approached with the mob seeking to capture Jesus. The disciples' sense of shock is clearly conveyed in the exclamation Matthew employs to describe Judas's sudden appearance on the scene: "*Behold, Judas . . .* with a great multitude with swords and clubs, came from the chief priests and elders of the people" (Matthew 26:47, emphasis added).

Judas's facade of faithfulness to Christ makes his treachery particularly heinous. The insidiousness of a close friend who pretended loyalty and love for Christ while betraying Him is far worse than if Christ had been handed over by someone known to be an enemy.

Judas's action is shown to be even more shameful by the fact that he brought a large mob armed with swords and clubs. They were prepared for violence. They were set to do bodily harm to Christ and the disciples, if necessary. And this was not an impromptu mob of citizens, but a hand-selected band of thugs carefully organized by the chief priests and elders.

Luke says the mob included members of the temple guard ("captains of the temple"—Luke 22:52). These were security officers who acted as policemen in the temple grounds and also had limited powers (sanctioned even by Rome) to arrest people for violations of the Jewish law (cf. John 7:32). On at least one prior occasion, the chief priests had ordered the captains of the temple to arrest Jesus, but when they heard Him teach, they were so confounded by the way He spoke with authority that they came back stunned and empty-handed (John 7:45–46).

John notes that the mob also included a detachment of Roman soldiers (John 18:3). Since the arrest of Jesus had been orchestrated by the Sanhedrin, they must have been the ones who requested the soldiers to participate in taking Jesus. Obviously they planned to try Him on capital charges, and since only Rome had authority to carry out the death penalty, it was necessary to have a contingent of soldiers involved at the time of the arrest. A garrison of Roman soldiers was permanently stationed at the Antonio Fortress, adjacent to the temple mount. These soldiers were no doubt sent from there. In order to gain the army's support in capturing Jesus, the chief priests had probably told the Roman authorities that Jesus was an anti-Roman insurrectionist.

None of the gospels gives a numerical estimate of the size of the mob, but Matthew, Mark, and Luke all agree that it was a great multitude (cf. Mark 14:43; Luke 22:47). Depending on the size of the detachment of soldiers (there were six hundred soldiers in a typical Roman cohort), the crowd could easily have numbered in the hundreds. The fact that the chief priests sent such a large crowd to make the arrest indicates the degree to which they were frightened of Jesus' power. Many times before this they had sought to arrest Him or silence Him, and their schemes had always been foiled. Jesus Himself called attention to their absurd and cowardly tactic of sending an armed multitude to arrest Him in the middle of the night. "Have you come out, as against a robber, with swords and clubs to take Me? I sat daily with you, teaching in the temple, and you did not seize Me" (Matthew 26:55). Such a large group was clearly overkill.

It was also unnecessary. They would face no resistance from Jesus. Of course, if He had *not* been willing to be arrested, no amount of earthly force would have been sufficient to capture Him. If it were not now His time in the perfect plan of God, He could easily have escaped even from such a large mob, as Jesus pointed out to Peter (v. 53).

THE EVIL DEED IS DONE

It had been a few hours at most since Judas left the Upper Room. It was already dark outside when he left, and by the time he arrived with the band of armed men it could not have been much later than midnight. Obviously he had gone directly from the Upper Room to the chief priests. Ever since they had paid him the blood money, he had been seeking an "opportunity to betray Him to them in the absence of the multitude" (Luke 22:6). Now, just in case, the conspirators decided to bring with them a multitude of their own. It would obviously have taken some time to round up such a crowd. But the readiness with which they were able to assemble so many temple guards, armed soldiers, and others shows their level of determination. Who knows what they had told the Roman authorities in order to get an immediate detachment of troops like this? It is clear that they had falsely made Jesus out to be a serious threat to Roman interests.

Judas was well familiar with the location of Gethsemane, having been there many times in recent days with Jesus (John 18:2). Perhaps that evening's trip to Gethsemane had been planned and discussed ahead of time among the disciples. Or maybe it was such a well-established habit that Judas simply knew where Jesus would go after supper. In any case, Judas must have been fairly certain Jesus would be there, to have brought such a large crowd along with him. As far as the conspirators were concerned, it was an ideal place to arrest Jesus without arousing the notice of the multitudes.

It would have been very dark in Gethsemane at that hour. Passover always fell on a full moon, so it was brighter than most nights, but in an olive grove the moonlight would barely provide enough light to make dim shadows in the darkness. So Judas had previously arranged a signal by which he would identify Jesus for his fellow conspirators.

Judas may have also feared that one of the disciples would surrender to the authorities in Jesus' place, pretending to be Him in order to spare His life. After all, just hours before in the Upper Room, Judas had listened while each of the other disciples had professed his willingness to go to prison or die for Christ (cf. John 13:37; Luke 22:33). Therefore to be certain that they could distinguish Jesus from the others, the conspirators had set up their prearranged signal. Judas had told them, "Whomever I kiss, He is the One; seize Him" (Matthew 26:48). The kiss in that culture was a sign of respect and homage as well as affection. Slaves kissed the feet of their masters as the utmost sign of respect. Disciples sometimes kissed the hem of their teacher's garment, as a token of reverence and deep devotion. It was common to kiss someone on the hand as a gesture of respect and honor. But a kiss on the face, especially with an embrace, signified personal friendship and affection. The gesture was reserved for the closest of friends, so that a disciple would not ordinarily embrace and kiss his teacher unless the teacher first offered the kiss.

The word Matthew employs to describe Judas's kiss is *kataphileo*, which means, "to kiss earnestly, intensively, or repeatedly." (It is the same word used to describe the affectionate worship lavished on Jesus by the woman at the Pharisee's house who anointed His feet with fragrant oil, wiped them with her hair, and repeatedly kissed *[kataphileo]* them—Luke 7:38.) As if it weren't enough for Judas to betray Jesus, in doing so he pretended the utmost affection, making his act even more despicable. Still under Satan's control, Judas evidently knew no shame. He could have chosen any signal for identifying Christ to his fellow conspirators. He deliberately chose one that compounded his own guilt with the most diabolical kind of hypocrisy. He seems to have deliberately drawn out his kissing in order to detain Jesus as long as possible, to be sure that the soldiers had time to apprehend Him.

Jesus' reply to Judas's false display of affection conveys a tone of sadness, but no malice or hostility: "Friend, why have you come?" (Matthew 26:50). There is a note of restraint and possibly aloofness in the expression. Christ did not employ the normal word for "friend." It was not *philos,* the word He used in the Upper Room when He told the disciples, "You are My friends if you do whatever I command you. No longer do I call you servants, for a servant does not know what his master is doing; but I have called you friends" (John 15:14–15). When he addressed Judas He used the word *hetairos,* meaning, "comrade," or "companion." Nonetheless, there is an irony in the fact that when Peter, a true friend, tried to impede Jesus' advance to the cross, Jesus addressed him as "Satan" (Matthew 16:22–23). But here Judas— a willing tool of Satan, indwelt and controlled by the prince of darkness himself—hands Jesus over to those who would crucify Him, and Jesus addresses him only as "comrade."

He asks, "Why have you come?" not because He did not know. But He wanted Judas to face up to—and the other disciples to recognize—what an evil thing Judas was doing. Luke records that He said, "Judas, are you betraying the Son of Man with a kiss?" (Luke 22:48). Even at this late hour, when Judas's heart was so obviously hardened against Christ, there is still an obvious tenderness in the way Jesus dealt with him. He uttered no invective; He did not speak harshly to Judas or call him names that would have been perfectly fitting, like *villain, infidel, traitor,* or *fool.* Instead, He addressed him as a comrade, called him by his name, and gently asked questions that would have smitten the conscience of anyone who was not utterly hardened. Judas's perfidy, set against the backdrop of Jesus' tenderness, looks all the more wicked.

But Judas was not deterred. He did not break stride. With bold-faced treachery, he handed Jesus over to His executioners, still pretending affection yet nurturing the most diabolical hatred in his heart.

Later Judas would have deep regret over what he had done (Matthew 27:4–5). But even then his regret was devoid of any true repentance. Having sold himself to Satan for thirty pieces of silver, he had already doomed himself to an eternity apart from the Holy One whom he so callously betrayed. It would have been better for him if he had not been born (Matthew 26:24).

A SLAUGHTER IS AVERTED

At least two of the disciples were armed. Having heard all Jesus' talk of betrayal and His predictions about His arrest and crucifixion, the disciples did not go into the garden unarmed. Earlier that evening in the Upper Room, when Jesus was informing them that one of them would betray Him, Luke records an exchange that took place:

> He said to them, "When I sent you without money bag, knapsack, and sandals, did you lack anything?" So they said, "Nothing." Then He said to them, "But now, he who has a money bag, let him take it, and likewise a knapsack; and he who has no sword, let him sell his garment and buy one. For I say to you that this which is written must still be accomplished in Me: 'And He was numbered with the transgressors.' For the things concerning Me have an end." So they said, "Lord, look, here are two swords." And He said to them, "It is enough." (Luke 22:35–38)

Christ was simply cautioning them about the impending violence. Although they had always been perfectly safe under God's providential care, a horrific act of violence was about to be perpetrated against them. They needed to prepare themselves for it so that when it occurred, their faith would not be shaken. He was speaking, of course, about spiritual, not physical, preparedness. He was warning them of a spiritual battle they were about to face, and He certainly was not telling them to arm themselves with fleshly weapons (2 Corinthians 10:4). But the disciples mistakenly assumed that He literally meant for them to go and purchase swords. So they had taken a private inventory and found that they already had two swords among them. Jesus' ambiguous reply ("It is enough") probably meant "enough of such talk." They may have thought He meant two swords were sufficient. In any case, His remark served its purpose and they thought no more about arming themselves further.

There was nothing unusual about Galilean fishermen carrying swords. These were long double-edged knives or daggers rather than full-length fighting swords. They were carried in a leather sheath strapped to the belt, and they had numerous practical uses other than violence against other people.

Of course, two weapons of that sort would be practically useless against an armed mob that included so many Roman soldiers. But the disciples, whose Messianic expectations no doubt still included the hope that Christ would rise up, overthrow Rome, and establish His throne in Jerusalem, may have been thinking He might use supernatural means to give the little band of disciples a miraculous military victory that night. And when they realized that Jesus was about to be taken by force, they asked, "Lord, shall we strike with the sword?" (Luke 22:49).

They were undoubtedly emboldened by something only John reports. When the attackers announced that they were seeking Jesus of Nazareth, "Jesus said to them, 'I am He.'. . . Now when He said to them, 'I am He,' they drew back and fell to the ground"

(John 18:5–6). Such a display of supernatural power may have spurred the disciples' thinking that Jesus planned to destroy His attackers supernaturally. So they asked Him if they should use their weapons.

Except for Peter. He saw no point in thinking or talking at this point. John tells us, "Simon Peter, having a sword, drew it and struck the high priest's servant, and cut off his right ear. The servant's name was Malchus" (v. 10). (Only John identifies Peter as the swordsman. It may be because the synoptic gospels were written much earlier, before Rome sacked Jerusalem and destroyed the temple. The synoptic writers may have refrained from identifying Peter because of the potential of reprisal from the Jewish leaders.)

Malchus was in all likelihood a high-ranking servant of the high priest, because he was apparently positioned at the front of the mob, an easy target for Peter. Peter was undoubtedly slashing at his neck or literally trying to split his skull, but Malchus flinched and Peter's blow glanced off the side of his head, severing the ear.

The cause of Christ has never been advanced by earthly warfare, though many misguided souls have tried. When such tactics are employed, they invariably hurt our Christian witness rather than helping it. The kingdom of God cannot be enlarged by physical weapons or worldly strategies. As Jesus told Pilate, "My kingdom is not of this world. If My kingdom were of this world, My servants would fight, so that I should not be delivered to the Jews; but now My kingdom is not from here" (John 18:36).

Jesus severely rebuked Peter: "Put your sword into the sheath" (John 18:11). Matthew says He added, "for all who take the sword will perish by the sword" (Matthew 26:52). The words were an echo of Genesis 9:6: "Whoever sheds man's blood, by man his blood shall be shed." Jesus was signifying that He regarded Peter's deed as no legitimate act of self-defense, but rather an unlawful act of attempted murder, worthy of punishment by death. Even though the arrest of Jesus was an unjust, cowardly act, it was being done by the duly established authorities in Jerusalem and therefore was not to be resisted with unlawful force (cf. Romans 13:2). Acts of violence or civil disobedience by an individual against duly constituted governments are always wrong, even if the government itself is unjust. (This is a point that needs to be reemphasized in an era when many Christians feel they are justified in breaking the law to protest government-sanctioned wrongs.)

Our Lord was not forbidding self-defense or defense of one's loved ones from every kind of violent attacker. He was not sanctioning any kind of radical pacifism. He was simply establishing the importance of submission to divinely ordained authority, even when that authority is unjust or abusive. Therefore he admonished Peter, "Permit even this" (Luke 22:51).

Christ had no need of fleshly power to defend Him anyway. He had already made that point in a graphic way when His mere words caused His attackers to stagger and fall to the ground. He continued His rebuke of Peter, "Do you think that I cannot now pray to My Father, and He will provide Me with more than twelve legions of angels?" (Matthew 26:53). A legion was comprised of 6,000 soldiers. Twelve angelic legions would be 72,000 angels. Bear in mind that in the Old Testament—when Sennacherib's armies threatened Jerusalem—a single angel slew 185,000 Assyrian troops in one night (2 Kings 19:35). So the military might of 72,000 angels would be quite imposing! If Christ had intended to be rescued from this armed mob, He certainly would not have needed Peter's sword.

But, he reminded Peter, He had a higher purpose. "How then could the Scriptures be fulfilled, that it must happen thus?" (Matthew 26:54). If angels rescued Him at this point, His atoning work could not be accomplished. "Shall I not drink the cup which My Father has given Me?" (John 18:11).

Christ had already shown them that the Scriptures would be fulfilled by Judas's betrayal (Psalm 41:9), as well as the smiting of the Shepherd that would scatter the sheep (Zechariah 13:7). There were numerous other Scriptures about the Messiah's suffering for sin that yet awaited fulfillment, and Christ was determined to see the fulfillment of them all. Once again, Peter's rash intervention was a fleshly impediment to the plan of God. "The anger of man does not achieve the righteousness of God" (James 1:20, NASB). "For the weapons of our warfare are not carnal" (2 Corinthians 10:4).

Malchus's severed ear was apparently still dangling from the side of his head. In a remarkable display of Jesus' power, "He touched his ear and healed him" (Luke 22:51). This is the only incident recorded in Scripture where Christ healed a fresh wound. It is all the more remarkable for the fact that Malchus was an unbeliever, hostile to Christ. But perhaps the most remarkable fact is that the miracle was virtually ignored by the mob. They carried on with their evil business as if nothing out of the ordinary had happened (v. 54). The healing of Malchus's ear had no more effect on their hearts than the powerful force that had knocked them to the ground a few moments before. They were like the men of Sodom who were struck blind by the power of God yet remained stubbornly undaunted in their evil quest (Genesis 19:10–11). Even a miraculous display of God's power would not deter them from the evil goal they had set their hearts on.

THE DISCIPLES FLEE

It was at this point that Jesus said to the mob, "Have you come out, as against a robber, with swords and clubs to take Me? I sat daily with you, teaching in the temple, and you did not seize Me" (Matthew 26:55). The cowardly way they came out against Jesus in the dead of night was proof that they knew they had no legitimate grounds for arresting Him. He was involved in no clandestine insurrection. He had done His teaching publicly and in broad daylight, usually on the temple grounds, in full view of everyone. If there had been lawful grounds for arresting Him, He could have been taken into custody on almost any day during that previous week. The Sanhedrin knew, of course, that such a public arrest could stir the crowd. That is why they had conspired to arrest Jesus secretly. But by saying this, Jesus exposed their subterfuge to the Roman soldiers who probably knew nothing about the Jewish leaders' real motives.

He added, "But all this was done, that the Scriptures of the prophets might be fulfilled" (v. 56). Thus Christ again sounds the refrain that is the constant theme of all four gospel accounts of the crucifixion. Despite their hostility to Christ, the men who arrested Him were fulfilling His sovereign purposes perfectly. Their attempts to destroy Him were only achieving *His* chosen ends, fulfilling a plan that was established before time began. His Word and His will would be fulfilled no matter how fiercely the powers of darkness sought to destroy Him.

The disciples had repeatedly heard Jesus express such absolute confidence in the sovereign plan of God. But under these circumstances, and at this moment, it seemed scant comfort to them. Christ had now been betrayed into the hands of His enemies. There was nothing they could do to stop it. They had never been in any situation that appeared so hopeless—at least not while they were in Jesus' presence. It had been a difficult few hours, and now utter despair set in. Their eyes were fixed firmly on the circumstances of the moment, not on the doctrine of God's sovereignty. And therefore they could draw no comfort from Jesus' reassuring words. Fear began to overwhelm them. "Then all the disciples forsook Him and fled" (v. 56).

Remember that even their desertion occurred so that the Scriptures might be fulfilled. They were acting precisely as Jesus said they would. If they reflected on these things at all, they must have realized that not one disaster had befallen them that He had not previously warned them about.

The disciples literally scattered, rather than fleeing as a group. Peter and John secretly followed the mob to the high priest's house (John 18:15). Nothing is said about where the other disciples went—but they apparently went into hiding.

In fairness to them, we should note that they all would indeed have been arrested or worse if they had stayed in the garden. That fact is evident from Jesus' plea to the arresting officers, recorded in John's account: "If you seek Me, let these go their way" (John 18:8). According to John, Jesus said that "[So] that the saying might be fulfilled which He spoke, 'Of those whom You gave Me I have lost none'" (v. 9). Probably when they heard Jesus say those words, they seized the moment and fled without hesitation.

Mark includes a vignette found in none of the other gospels: "They all forsook Him and fled. Now a certain young man followed Him, having a linen cloth thrown around his naked body. And the young men laid hold of him, and he left the linen cloth and fled from them naked" (Mark 14:50–52). Who that "certain young man" was is nowhere stated, but it may well have been Mark himself. The "young men" who laid hold of him were no doubt the Roman soldiers. Whoever this unnamed young man was, he had apparently been in bed, or preparing for bed, when the noise of the mob awakened him. Without taking time to dress, he threw on a linen cloth, perhaps a bedsheet, and followed the noise to see what was happening. Assuming that he was a follower of Christ, the soldiers tried to apprehend him. He escaped, but only by abandoning his makeshift clothing and fleeing into the night naked.

This certainly proves that the disciples themselves were indeed in danger that night.

And so they all deserted their Master. But He was by no means alone. Jesus had earlier told the disciples, "Indeed the hour is coming, yes, has now come, that you will be scattered, each to his own, and will leave Me alone. And yet I am not alone, because the Father is with Me" (John 16:32).

The divine work of redemption thus continued on schedule. Christ's sovereign plan would be fulfilled in every detail, despite the opposition of His enemies—and even despite the abandonment of His friends.

6

They twist my words; all their thoughts are against me
for evil.

—PSALM 56:5

6

 The Kangaroo Court of the High Priest

CHRIST WAS TAKEN from Gethsemane directly to Annas, the former high priest, who still wielded the power of the high priest's office (John 18:13). Annas had Him bound and sent Him to the home of Caiaphas, his son-in-law, who was the official high priest at the time (v. 24). Caiaphas convened a hasty meeting of the Sanhedrin, and Christ was immediately put on trial in the middle of the night. The charges against Him were trumped up, and the witnesses against Him were bribed. The entire trial was a complete mockery of justice. By all the biblical standards that were supposed to govern the dispensation of justice in Israel, the trial was illegal and its verdict unjust.

The fundamental standards of justice in Israel were established by the divine law given to Moses. The system of justice God had established in Israel was designed to ensure maximum fairness and to encourage mercy. In fact, the standards of Moses' law when instituted were a dramatic advancement in civil and criminal justice. Moses' system was far and away superior to any of the Canaanite standards. It was also more advanced and more equitable than the Egyptian justice system. In fact, the standards established by the Mosaic law are the whole basis of our modern notions of justice.

Deuteronomy 16:18–20 set forth the basic principles of jurisprudence in Israel:

> You shall appoint judges and officers in all your gates, which the LORD your God gives you, according to your tribes, and they shall judge the people with just judgment. You shall not pervert justice; you shall not show partiality, nor take a bribe, for a bribe blinds the eyes of the wise and twists the words of the righteous. You shall follow what is altogether just, that you may live and inherit the land which the LORD your God is giving you.

In the Old Testament era, local courts were managed by local authorities. Justice was both swift and fair, because it was administered within the community by both the leaders and the people of the community. Israel was a theocracy, with God as King mediating His rule through the revelation of His Word. Under that theocratic government, civil law and religious law were inextricably intertwined, so that those with the most expertise in Scripture were deemed legal experts. When the New Testament uses the term "lawyers," it is speaking of men who were Old Testament scholars, experts in *Moses'* law. The civil justice system was therefore governed first of all by biblical principles.

Sometime after the Babylonian Captivity, probably during the Maccabean period (between the Old and New Testaments), the Great Sanhedrin was established in Jerusalem as the highest court in Israel. (There were smaller groups also called Sanhedrin that functioned as courts in many local communities, but the Great Sanhedrin in Jerusalem served as Israel's Supreme Court.) The Great Sanhedrin was patterned after the council of elders Moses convened in Numbers 11:16: "The LORD said to Moses: "Gather to Me seventy men of the elders of Israel, whom you know to be the elders of the people and officers over them; bring them to the tabernacle of meeting, that they may stand there with you." Those seventy men, plus Moses, formed a council of seventy-one elders whose job it was to govern the Israelites in the wilderness.

Since Moses' council of elders was the pattern for the Sanhedrin, that council also numbered seventy-one—comprised of twenty-four chief priests (the heads of the twenty-four priestly divisions, cf. 1 Chronicles 24:4, Revelation 4:4) plus forty-six more elders chosen from among the scribes, Pharisees, and Sadducees. The high priest was both the overseer and a voting member of the Sanhedrin, bringing the number to seventy-one. (The odd number ensured that decisions could be reached by majority vote.)

By Jesus' time, the Sanhedrin had become a corrupt and politically motivated body. Appointment to the council could be bought with political favors and sometimes even with money. Favoritism and partisanship were therefore rife, and political expediency often determined who rose to power or fell from it within the Sanhedrin. Rome exercised ultimate control over the high priesthood, because Rome could appoint or depose the high priest. Both the high priest and the ruling priests of the temple were all Sadducees, who openly denied the supernatural elements of the Old Testament. Constant political tensions seethed between the various factions of the Sanhedrin, the people of Israel, Rome, and Herod. Therefore the Sanhedrin often made decisions that were politically motivated. In fact, aside from their obvious religious animosity to the teaching of Christ, sheer political expediency was the motive for conspiring to carry out the arrest and crucifixion of Christ (see John 11:47–53).

Despite the corruption within the Sanhedrin, the justice system was still governed by rules of evidence and principles of impartiality that had been established under Moses. Two credible witnesses were still required to establish guilt. The accused were supposed to be entitled to a public trial. People placed on trial were entitled to a defense, including the right to call witnesses and present evidence.

As a deterrent to anyone who might bring false testimony against an accused person, Moses' law established this principle:

> If a false witness rises against any man to testify against him of wrong-doing, then both men in the controversy shall stand before the LORD, before the priests and the judges who serve in those days. And the judges shall make careful inquiry, and indeed, if the witness is a false witness, who has testified falsely against his brother, then you shall do to him as he thought to have done to his brother; so you shall put away the evil from among you. (Deuteronomy 19:16–19)

So if someone testified falsely against a person accused of a capital crime, the false witness himself could be given the death penalty.

Rabbinical tradition had added another restriction on death-penalty cases. A full day of fasting had to be observed by the council between the passing of sentence and the execution of the criminal. (That not only prevented hasty trials and executions, but it also kept capital cases off the docket during the feasts.) After the obligatory day of fasting, council members were polled again to see if they had changed their opinions. Guilty verdicts could thus be overturned, but a not-guilty verdict could not be rescinded.

All those principles were established to ensure that trials were both fair and merciful. Legal scholars who have studied the justice system of the Sanhedrin cite numerous other principles that governed the hearing of capital cases. To ensure fairness, the council could try cases only where an outside party had brought the charges.

If charges had been brought against the accused by council members, the entire council was disqualified from trying the case. Testimony of all witnesses had to be precise as to the date, time, and location of the event one was testifying about. Women, children, slaves, and the mentally incompetent were not permitted to testify. Persons of questionable character were also disqualified from being witnesses. The accused was to be presumed innocent until an official guilty verdict was reached. Criminal trials were not to be convened at night, and if a trial was already underway when nighttime fell, court was to be recessed until the following day.

Nearly all those principles were openly flouted in the trial of Christ. His trial was unjust and illegal by virtually every principle of jurisprudence that was known at the time. Caiaphas and the Sanhedrin turned their own council into a kangaroo court with the predetermined purpose of killing Jesus. The trial they imposed on Him was one extended act of deliberate inhumanity, the greatest miscarriage of justice in the history of the world.

A COWARDLY NIGHTTIME TRIAL

Matthew writes, "And those who had laid hold of Jesus led Him away to Caiaphas the high priest, where the scribes and the elders were assembled. But Peter followed Him at a distance to the high priest's courtyard" (Matthew 26:57–58). The apostle John's account fills in more details. John apparently followed Jesus to the high priest's house too (John 18:15). And from John we learn that before Jesus was taken to Caiaphas's house, "they led Him away to Annas first, for he was the father-in-law of Caiaphas who was high priest that year" (v. 13).

Annas was one of the most powerful men in Jerusalem. He had served as high priest twenty years before this (A.D. 7–14), and for all practical purposes, he had controlled the high priest's office ever since. Five of his sons had already succeeded him as High Priest, and now his son-in-law, Caiaphas, had the title. Annas thus managed to control the high priesthood through his sons and son-in-law until the end of his life. As the real power behind the office, he also retained use of the title. Therefore several times in the New Testament, he is referred to as the high priest (cf. Luke 3:2).

Annas and family had managed to turn the high priesthood into an incredibly profitable business, and they had amassed enormous wealth through it. They did this chiefly by collecting license fees and commissions from the brokers who changed money and sold sacrificial animals on the temple grounds. The entire business was crooked. Both the moneychangers and the animal merchants were renowned for their dishonesty and greed. Since Annas controlled a monopoly on the whole enterprise, the merchants who worked for him could charge exorbitant rates—especially during the seasons of the feasts when the city was filled with pilgrims. Of course Annas himself took a hefty portion of the profits. Thus Annas and his sons had grown wealthy at the expense of people who came to worship God. That explains Jesus' outrage over the whole business, which led Him to purge the temple by driving out the moneychangers and animal sellers on two occasions (Matthew 21:12–13; Mark 11:15–17; John 2:14–16).

Why were moneychangers at the temple in the first place? Because the Roman coins that were used in most commerce had an image of Caesar stamped on them, and that was deemed idolatrous (cf. Matthew 22:20–21). Roman coins were therefore not to be used for donations to the temple treasury. Worshipers coming to the temple were required to use Jewish coins for their tithes, almsgiving, and temple taxes. Ostensibly for the sake of convenience, moneychangers licensed by the high priest were permitted to ply their trade right on the temple grounds, exchanging foreign currencies for Jewish coins. But the exchange rate they offered was unreasonably disadvantageous to the worshiper. In short, the high priest was sanctioning a form of organized larceny.

Something similar was happening with the animal trade at the temple and elsewhere around Jerusalem. Worshipers were required to bring an unblemished animal—and the priests certified animals as to their fitness for sacrificial purposes. All the temple brokers' animals were precertified for sacrificial purposes. Therefore it was often much easier for out-of-town worshipers to purchase an animal at or near the temple, rather than bringing one's own animal from a distance only to have it disqualified when the temple priest found a blemish of some kind. As high priest, Annas virtually owned the franchise on precertified sacrificial animals. He and the merchants who worked for him took full advantage of this situation and fixed unreasonably high prices on the precertified animals both at the temple mount and throughout the city of Jerusalem.

Annas administered this power through his sons, who regularly collected the high priest's cut of profits from those shady businesses. Annas functioned very much like a modern organized crime boss. No wonder Christ twice purged the temple. Annas had quite literally turned it into a house of merchandise and a den of thieves (John 2:16; Mark 11:17).

And no wonder Annas was so determined to eliminate Christ. Jesus had repeatedly been a threat to Annas's business interests. Moreover, Christ was everything a true high priest should have been—holy, devout, chaste, honorable, and virtuous. Corrupt men who wield power as Annas did simply cannot abide true righteousness. Jesus was a constant rebuke to Annas. For all those reasons Annas had to see Him destroyed.

The fact that those who arrested Jesus first brought Him to Annas proves that Annas himself was the ultimate power behind the plot to kill Jesus. He ultimately had to authorize the deed, and without his sanction the evil plot never would have gone forward. Also, the fact that the conspirators took Him to Annas before they went to Caiaphas reveals the true nature of Caiaphas's high priesthood. He was virtually a puppet, under his father-in-law's control.

The hearing at Annas's house was evidently held for one purpose: to trump up a specific charge against Jesus. The plan was for Annas to listen to Jesus give an account of His teaching, and then Annas would decide what kind of charge to file. He had several options at his disposal. He could charge Jesus with blasphemy, a crime punishable by death under Jewish law. Since Jesus had said many things in His public ministry that the Jewish leaders deemed blasphemous, that seemed the most likely charge.

But the Romans, who must authorize and carry out all executions, rarely approved of the death penalty for blasphemy. For that reason Annas might also look for a way to charge Jesus with sedition or insurrection. Understandably, Rome was not inclined to be merciful to anti-Roman agitators.

While Jesus was taken before Annas, Caiaphas would have time to gather the Sanhedrin at his house for the impromptu trial (Matthew 26:57). The speed with which he was able to do this reveals the entire council's eagerness to do away with Jesus.

John records that Annas "asked Jesus about His disciples and His doctrine" (John 18:19). In effect, Jesus was being arraigned (brought before a court to answer charges), even though He had not yet been indicted (formally charged with a specific offense). This was completely out of order and contrary to every standard of fair jurisprudence. Moreover, Annas was in effect trying to get Jesus to implicate Himself—and that was also contrary to the principles of justice that were supposed to govern the Sanhedrin.

But Jesus' reply subtly exposed the illegality of Annas's line of questioning: "I spoke openly to the world. I always taught in synagogues and in the temple, where the Jews always meet, and in secret I have said nothing. Why do you ask Me? Ask those who have heard Me what I said to them. Indeed they know what I said" (John 18:20–21). He was not being impertinent. He had no legal obligation to testify against Himself, particularly before any charges were filed against Him. Annas was supposed to state the charges against Jesus before he could cross-examine Him in a hearing of this sort. Since no specific charges had been brought against Him, it was not Jesus' obligation to supply Annas with information he might later employ to incriminate Him. Annas, of course, knew this.

Nonetheless, "when He had said these things, one of the officers who stood by struck Jesus with the palm of his hand, saying, 'Do You answer the high priest like that?'" (v. 22). The officer's action was probably meant to cover the high priest's embarrassment. It may also have been a deliberate attempt to rankle Jesus, to try to goad Him into an angry retort that could be used against Him.

But Jesus retained His composure perfectly. "[He] answered him, 'If I have spoken evil, bear witness of the evil; but if well, why do you strike Me?'" (v. 23). If Jesus had spoken blasphemy or tried to foment revolution, it was His accusers' responsibility to give a detailed account and proof of His wrongdoing. If they had no knowledge of any crimes He could be charged with, they had no right to hold Him, much less strike Him.

Annas was clearly embarrassed by Jesus' response. Christ had exposed the high priest's ruse without giving him any information that would help in the trumping up of charges. Exasperated and still unable to find anything he could charge Jesus with, Annas finally had Him bound and sent Him to Caiaphas's house, where members of the Sanhedrin were already assembled for the trial.

The homes of Annas and Caiaphas apparently shared a common courtyard. It was typical in that culture for sons and sons-in-law to build homes adjacent to or attached to the parents' home. Between the homes would be a courtyard, and apparently it was in such a courtyard that Peter and John stood, warming their hands on a fire of coals while waiting to see the results of the hearing (John 18:15–18). John "was known to the high priest" (v. 16), which probably reflects his family's social status. John therefore gained admittance to the courtyard for Peter as well. So when Matthew reports that Peter was in *Caiaphas's* courtyard with the servants, awaiting the outcome of the trial (Matthew 26:58), it is probably the same place John spoke of next to Annas's house where the servants had built a coal fire. That also means when Annas sent Jesus bound to Caiaphas, it was a very short procession—probably taking Jesus through the very same courtyard where Peter and John were waiting.

The fact that formal charges had not yet been filed against Jesus was probably an embarrassment and surely a frustration to the council, but it was ultimately no deterrent to their plans. They already had a cabal of false witnesses who were prepared to testify against Jesus.

SOLICITATION OF FALSE TESTIMONY

Matthew writes, "Now the chief priests, the elders, and all the council sought false testimony against Jesus to put Him to death, but found none. Even though many false witnesses came forward, they found none" (Matthew 26:59–60).

It was not the business of the council to solicit anyone's testimony. They were supposed to be acting in the capacity of impartial judges, not prosecuting attorneys. By openly soliciting damaging testimony against Jesus, they forfeited any perception of impartiality. But they probably believed that if their conspiracy against Jesus did not succeed now, it would never succeed. So they were desperate. They were determined to press the issue against Jesus until they found some reasonably credible complaint against Him—even if it meant destroying any vestige of legitimacy that might have been left in their illegal hearing.

The phrase "even though many false witnesses came forward, they found none" means that many people came forward who were willing to bear false witness against Jesus, but none were found credible enough to sustain a charge against Him. According to Mark, the false witnesses contradicted one another: "Their testimonies did not agree" (Mark 14:56). They couldn't even find liars who were clever enough to fabricate a tale that agreed with the lies of others.

But finally two false witnesses came forward and said, "This fellow said, 'I am able to destroy the temple of God and to build it in three days'" (Matthew 26:60–61). Mark's account sheds even more light on what these false witnesses were claiming: "We heard Him say, 'I will destroy this temple made with hands, and within three days I will build another made without hands'" (Mark 14:58). Mark adds, "But not even then did their testimony agree" (v. 59). The details of their stories still didn't quite jibe—but there were enough similarities in what they said to give their testimony a veneer of credibility. One witness apparently claimed he had heard Christ say if the temple were torn down, He would be able to rebuild it in three days (Matthew 26:61). The other claimed what He actually said was that He *would* destroy the temple and rebuild a new temple made without hands (Mark 14:58).

They both were obviously referring to a statement Jesus had made early in His ministry, after He cleansed the temple the first time. Here is John's account of what really happened:

So the Jews answered and said to Him, "What sign do You show to us, since You do these things?" Jesus answered and said to them, "Destroy this temple, and in three days I will raise it up." Then the Jews said, "It has taken forty-six years to build this temple, and will You raise it up in three days?" But He was speaking of the temple of His body. (John 2:18–21)

The incident actually took place at Passover in the first year of Jesus' public ministry—three years to the day before this trial at Caiaphas's house. Most of Jesus' hearers on that occasion wrongly assumed that He was speaking of the destruction of the actual temple. His meaning was deliberately ambiguous, and only after the resurrection did the disciples fully understand that the saying was a reference to the temple of His body (v. 21). But most of the crowd assumed He was speaking about the Jerusalem temple (v. 20). The two witnesses at Caiaphas's house had evidently both been present that day three years before, and they had not forgotten the incident, even though neither was able to give a precise account of what Jesus really claimed. The inconsistency in their testimony shows how badly Jesus' words were misunderstood by the people who originally heard Him.

But the testimony of those two witnesses nonetheless served Caiaphas's purposes. The testimony could be twisted to suggest that Jesus was advocating the total overthrow of the Jewish religion (by replacing the current temple with another). Furthermore, the Sanhedrin could charge Him with high blasphemy for claiming that He could rebuild the temple by miraculous means ("without hands"—Mark 14:58). After all, Herod's temple had been under construction for forty-six years (John 2:20), and although it was not yet completely finished, it was already one of the most spectacular edifices in the world. So Jesus' claim probably seemed arrogant in the extreme to anyone who assumed he was speaking about destroying and rebuilding Herod's temple. Therefore it was this claim that Caiaphas focused on. He asked Jesus, "Do You answer nothing? What is it these men testify against You?" (Matthew 26:62).

A DESPERATE ATTEMPT TO GET JESUS TO INCRIMINATE HIMSELF

Since there were obvious discrepancies in the stories told by the witnesses, their testimony should have been automatically disallowed and the case against Jesus dismissed. But the Sanhedrin was obviously in no mood for that. They had already secretly determined to eliminate the threat they imagined Jesus posed to their power, and to do that, they needed credible evidence against Him. Now they seemed to have it—or at least these witnesses' testimony could be spun into something akin to proof that He was guilty of blasphemy. And so "the high priest arose and said to Him, 'Do You answer nothing? What is it these men testify against You?'" (Matthew 26:62).

Jesus responded with utter silence. It is easy to picture Him looking directly into Caiaphas's eyes with steely calm. He had no obligation to testify against Himself. And just as He had done previously with Annas, He made that point with Caiaphas in a dramatic way—by simply declining to testify against Himself. Centuries before, the prophet had foretold that very silence: "He was oppressed and He was afflicted, yet He opened not His mouth; He was led as a lamb to the slaughter, and as a sheep before its shearers is silent, so He opened not His mouth" (Isaiah 53:7).

Finally in frustration, Caiaphas charged Jesus with an oath: "I put You under oath by the living God: Tell us if You are the Christ, the Son of God!" (Matthew 26:63). Obviously Caiaphas was familiar with Jesus' claims. He knew that Jesus had publicly "said that God was His Father, making Himself equal with God" (John 5:18). Prior to this occasion, Jesus had repeatedly identified Himself as both Messiah (the Christ) and the Son of God (John 4:25–26; 9:35–37; Matthew 16:20). Claiming to be God certainly would have been sufficient grounds for charging any ordinary man with blasphemy, and blasphemy was a capital crime under Moses' law ("Whoever blasphemes the name of the LORD shall surely be put to death"—Leviticus 24:16.)

But Caiaphas still needed credible testimony to prove that Jesus had made such claims, and all he had was hearsay. The testimony of the two witnesses was also flawed. It would have to do, unless better evidence could be found. But before moving on, Caiaphas first placed Jesus under oath and demanded that He tell them whether He was Christ, the Son of God.

Jesus gave him precisely what he hoped for. He replied, "It is as you said. Nevertheless, I say to you, hereafter you will see the Son of Man sitting at the right hand of the Power, and coming on the clouds of heaven" (Matthew 26:64). Mark records that Jesus furthermore declared, "I am"—which was the proper name by which God revealed Himself to Moses (Exodus 3:13–14)—and thus provided personal testimony from the accused in support of the Sanhedrin's accusation that He claimed to be God. The promise of His coming on the clouds of heaven was another clear declaration of His Messiahship, an unmistakable reference to the well-known Messianic prophecy in Daniel 7:13–14:

I was watching in the night visions, and behold, One like the Son of Man, coming with the clouds of heaven! He came to the Ancient of Days, and they brought Him near before Him. Then to Him was given dominion and glory and a kingdom, that all peoples, nations, and languages should serve Him. His dominion is an everlasting dominion, which shall not pass away, and His kingdom the one which shall not be destroyed.

It was all Caiaphas needed to hear.

A PREDETERMINED VERDICT

Matthew 26:65–66 says, "Then the high priest tore his clothes, saying, 'He has spoken blasphemy! What further need do we have of witnesses? Look, now you have heard His blasphemy! What do you think?'" The tearing of Caiaphas's clothes was supposed to signify his utter shock and outrage over an alleged act of open blasphemy. Tearing one's clothes was an expression of extreme grief and shock from the most ancient biblical times (cf. Genesis 37:34; Numbers 14:6; 2 Samuel 1:11). However, the high priest was forbidden to tear his clothes (Leviticus 21:10). So ironically, while Annas was theatrically feigning indignation over Jesus' supposed act of blasphemy, he himself was actually committing a rather serious act of sacrilege, profaning the high priest's office in a way Scripture expressly forbids.

Caiaphas's artificial outrage reflected no genuine concern for the holiness of God's name. He must have been secretly overjoyed to hear Jesus say something he could accuse Him with. The exaggerated gesture of tearing his clothes would have barely disguised the glee on his face over the fact that he was finally able to get Jesus to make a statement that had the semblance of blasphemy—or would have if Jesus had been a mere man.

But Jesus was no mere man, and His claims were not blasphemy. The Sanhedrin erred seriously by ignoring the numerous miracles Jesus had done, many of them public acts that occurred in Jerusalem, right under their noses. In fact, years earlier in Galilee, on one of the first occasions when some Jewish religious leaders sought

Jesus' life for claiming God was His Father, He defended Himself with these words:

> If I bear witness of Myself, My witness is not true. There is another who bears witness of Me, and I know that the witness which He witnesses of Me is true. You have sent to John, and he has borne witness to the truth. Yet I do not receive testimony from man, but I say these things that you may be saved. He was the burning and shining lamp, and you were willing for a time to rejoice in his light. But I have a greater witness than John's; for the works which the Father has given Me to finish; the very works that I do; bear witness of Me, that the Father has sent Me. And the Father Himself, who sent Me, has testified of Me. (John 5:31–37)

Not only had John the Baptist borne witness that Jesus was the Messiah, but God the Father Himself had confirmed the fact through numerous miraculous works. The Sanhedrin knew of these things and had witnessed some of the miracles themselves. (As a matter of fact, the raising of Lazarus was the incident that had prompted this final, desperate conspiracy to murder Jesus—John 11:46–53.) But in their zeal to eliminate Christ they discounted all the evidence that supported His claims.

As the high priest tore his clothes, he said, "What further need do we have of witnesses? Look, now you have heard His blasphemy!" (Matthew 26:65). He now had the "evidence" he needed, and to his absolute delight there was no need for any testimony from witnesses to confirm it. As far as he was concerned, Christ had blasphemed openly before the entire council. They all were witnesses against Him. His condemnation was now a done deal. The high priest immediately asked for a verdict from the council: "What do you think?"

They dutifully answered, "He is deserving of death" (v. 66). And thus the council rendered a summary verdict: "They all condemned Him to be deserving of death" (Mark 14:64). It was the verdict they had agreed upon long before they ever heard His case.

No one was permitted to speak in His defense. No voice of caution was raised at any point in the trial. No plea for mercy was entertained. None of the evidence that supported His claims was ever considered. Jesus was simply railroaded by the high priest's kangaroo court into a guilty verdict that had been arranged and agreed upon long before He ever came to trial.

RUTHLESS CRUELTY

Finally having accomplished the evil goal they had so long sought, the members of the Sanhedrin began to vent their satanic hatred of Jesus openly. "They spat in His face and beat Him; and others struck Him with the palms of their hands, saying, "Prophesy to us, Christ! Who is the one who struck You?" (Matthew 26:67–68). According to Luke, they blindfolded Him before striking Him and ordering Him to prophesy about who hit Him. Luke adds that there were "many other things they blasphemously spoke against Him" (Luke 22:65). Ironically, blasphemy was the very crime they had accused Him of, but they themselves were the ones who were guilty of it.

Christ bore all such abuse with a quiet and majestic grace that is quite remarkable. As always, "when He was reviled, [He] did not revile in return; when He suffered, He did not threaten, but committed Himself to Him who judges righteously" (1 Peter 2:23). He would soon be bearing others' sins; meanwhile He also patiently suffered their hateful abuse.

Isaiah's prophecy, written at least seven hundred years earlier, perfectly described this moment. "He is despised and rejected by men, a Man of sorrows and acquainted with grief. And we hid, as it were, our faces from Him; He was despised, and we did not esteem Him" (Isaiah 53:3). Isaiah thus prophetically foretold the whole world's sinful apathy toward Jesus Christ. No one came to His defense. No one spoke in His favor. He was left to bear His affliction all alone.

And thus Christ was unjustly condemned to die. His trial before the Sanhedrin had gone exactly according to Caiaphas's evil plan. At the same time, the plan of God was right on schedule as well.

7

❦

Now Simon Peter stood and warmed himself. Therefore they said to him, "You are not also one of His disciples, are you?" He denied it and said, "I am not!"

—JOHN 18:25

7

 Peter's Denial

WHILE JESUS WAS INSIDE the high priest's house on trial for His life, Peter was just outside in the courtyard. He too was facing the trial of his life, but in a different sense. Satan was sifting him like wheat (Luke 22:31). The imagery of that expression refers to the violent shaking of a tray of grain, which causes the chaff to be thrown into the air and blown away with the wind, leaving behind pure kernels of grain.

God often permits us to be tested by various trials. The purifying process that results is essential—and for true believers, it is always ultimately beneficial (James 1:2–4). But the violent shaking required for the sifting process is inherently unsettling and often quite painful. In fact, as far as Peter was concerned, the pain of the purifying process was more analogous to the fiery heat of the smelter's crucible than the shaking of a tray of wheat. Years later, Peter would encourage others in the midst of the refiner's fire: "You greatly rejoice, though now for a little while, if need be, you have been grieved by various trials, that the genuineness of your faith, being much more precious than gold that perishes, though it is tested by fire, may be found to praise, honor, and glory at the revelation of Jesus Christ" (1 Peter 1:6–7).

Peter's trial certainly purified his faith—even despite his horrible failure. In years to come the memory of that awful night (and his subsequent restoration by a forgiving Master) would no doubt embolden him to face more and even greater trials without ever again denying Christ. In fact, Peter would ultimately forfeit his very life for Christ's sake (John 21:18–19).

But on that infamous final night of Jesus' earthly ministry, Peter experienced utter failure when put to the test. In the immediate aftermath of his spiritual collapse, it must have seemed to Peter as if no good thing could ever come from such shame and defeat. He probably assumed his ministry for Christ was finished forever. But Christ was not finished with Peter yet.

The story of Peter's denial is therefore a lesson about the security of God's saving grace. In fact, what is emphasized most in Scripture throughout this account is not Peter's *failure,* but the Lord's *forgiveness.* The reason the episode is recounted for us in such detail in Scripture is not merely to remind us of our human frailty, but more important to reassure us of the wonderful security we have in Christ.

From the very beginning, when Christ first told Peter and the other disciples that Satan desired to sift them like wheat, He subtly assured them of the inevitable victory they would experience in the long term. He told them, "I have prayed for you, that your faith should not fail; and when you have returned to Me, strengthen your brethren" (Luke 22:32). Clearly, the disciples' temporary failure was just one more element in Jesus' perfect plan, and therefore He would ultimately use even this for good.

Because of the grace shown to them in the midst of their failure, the disciples were uniquely equipped to strengthen their brethren against similar failure. When waves of Roman persecution came against the early church in later years, many believers would be strongly tempted to deny or forsake Christ to save their own lives the same way the disciples had. The disciples, having all drunk deeply of the bitterness and sorrow that come from such defection, knew better than anyone how to encourage weak and fearful believers to remain faithful. Peter himself was used mightily by the Holy Spirit for that very purpose (1 Peter 3:14–17).

Moreover, during that dark night of Peter's trial, although his courage and devotion failed when put to the test, his faith in Christ did *not* fail. That is what distinguished the temporary defection of Peter and the other disciples from the treachery of Judas. Judas's disavowal of Christ was a deliberate, premeditated, full, and final rejection of Christ—an act of pure, hardhearted unbelief. But Peter's denial was a spur-of-the-moment act of weakhearted cowardice. Peter's fundamental faith in Christ remained intact throughout the trial and always afterward. What he did was certainly sinful, but it was not in the same league as Judas's treason.

Of course, Jesus knew Peter's denial was no hardhearted rejection of Him as Judas's betrayal had been. Therefore soon after His resurrection Jesus tenderly sought out Peter and forgave him in the presence of the other disciples. He then commissioned him anew for service (John 21:15–17). So the *final* chapter of the story is a great triumph, and not a defeat, for Peter.

But the chapter written that fateful night was a stunning defeat by any standard.

THE GROUNDWORK FOR FAILURE

How did Peter fall? It is important to see that his failure did not occur spontaneously. Peter himself took the wrong steps that put him on the pathway to failure. In order to examine those steps systematically, it is necessary to back up a bit in Matthew's narrative and review some already familiar ground.

He Boasted Too Loudly

Peter's first mistake was the boasting self-confidence he showed when Jesus first warned the disciples they were standing on the precipice of serious failure. Back in Matthew 26:31, Jesus told them, "All of you will be made to stumble because of Me this night, for it is written: 'I will strike the Shepherd, and the sheep of the flock will be scattered.'" Christ's words should have instantly sobered Peter and the others. A wise person would have been humbled—and would have begged the Lord for strength to resist such an imminent temptation.

But not Peter. He bragged, "Even if all are made to stumble because of You, I will never be made to stumble" (v. 33).

Peter, who often acted as spokesman for the whole group, seemed particularly prone to reckless impetuosity. He frequently spoke before he thought. On a few occasions, he was even so brash as to contradict Jesus—like the time in Mark 8:32 when Peter took Jesus aside and *rebuked* Him for saying He would be rejected by the Jewish leaders and killed. Peter no doubt meant well, but Jesus quickly let him know how far out of line such a rebuke was. He did so by addressing Peter as "Satan" (for Satan was behind Peter's words), and by reprimanding him for being too concerned about earthly things and not concerned enough for matters pertaining to the heavenly kingdom (v. 33).

Peter should have been listening more closely. If he had simply thought carefully about who Jesus is, he would have seen the folly of "correcting" Him in *any* context. In fact, it was utterly incongruous to confess (as Peter just had) that Jesus is the Christ, the Son of the Living God (Matthew 16:16), and then moments later turn around and rebuke Him for what He was teaching (v. 22). Unfortunately, Peter did not always seem to sense when he should be listening rather than sounding off.

To make matters worse, Peter (like all of us) sometimes neglected to learn from his own mistakes. Even after Jesus corrected him, he remained slow to hear and quick to speak. You would think with all his bitter experience, he would know by then not to argue with Christ. After all, Jesus had never been wrong about anything. But right up to the night of Jesus' betrayal—the last night of our Lord's earthly ministry and the very end of Peter's three-year discipleship—when Jesus tried to forewarn Peter and the disciples that they were about to stumble, Peter not only argued with Jesus, but he kept pressing the point even after Jesus corrected him. "Jesus said to him, 'Assuredly, I say to you that this night, before the rooster crows, you will deny Me three times.' Peter said to Him, 'Even if I have to die with You, I will not deny You!'" (Matthew 26:34–35).

There was simply no talking to Peter about it. He brashly assumed he knew his own heart even better than Jesus did. He kept right on *insisting* that he would never fall away, even if he were the last person in the world left standing for Christ.

But all the good intentions in the world do not equal real virtue. Boasting is no true measure of boldness. Peter's braggadocio proved only his folly, not his faithfulness. Genuine allegiance to Christ is best shown by being faithful under fire from the enemies of the gospel, not by a lot of swaggering, blustering words spoken to one's fellow believers.

Peter had no earthly idea of the severity of the trial he was about to undergo. That is what made his confident boasting especially inappropriate. In fact, such a boast was the *worst* response Peter could have made to the Lord's tender warning that he was about to fail. Peter ought to have listened rather than talked. He should have prayed for the Lord's help rather than asserted his own self-sufficiency. Boasting only inflamed his carnal pride. And pride was the whole basis of Peter's problem in the first place. The feeling of invincibility that caused him to boast was itself a manifestation of sinful pride.

Moreover, Peter was a victim of self-deception. The devotion to Christ he bragged about was little more than sheer emotion—a mere *feeling* of love and allegiance to Christ, without any genuine counting of the real cost. Peter evidently thought he had arrived at a level of spiritual maturity where his priorities were well fixed, his position as the leading disciple was firmly established, and he therefore thought himself incapable of serious failure. He was talking as if he were invulnerable to the onslaughts of Satan. He clearly could not envision any circumstance that would place him in any real spiritual peril. And so he foolishly convinced himself that Jesus was simply wrong. That is precisely the kind of "pride [that] goes before destruction, and a haughty spirit before a fall" (Proverbs 16:18; cf. 1 Corinthians 10:12). "Do not be haughty, but fear" (Romans 11:20).

He Prayed Too Little

Peter also erred because he neglected prayer. When Christ entered Gethsemane that night, He deliberately took Peter, James, and John deep into the garden with Him, and said, "Stay here and watch with Me" (Matthew 26:38). He desired them to pray with Him. Repeatedly He awakened them and urged them to pray with Him. It was for their sakes. They needed fortification and renewal of their strength far more than He did. But they did not sense their own need.

Prayer was the one thing that could have strengthened Peter to face the temptation the Lord had forewarned him about. But having already scorned Jesus' warning about his imminent failure, Peter had no sense of his desperate need to pray for God to strengthen him.

I'm convinced that most of the problems and failures Christians face are directly related to prayerlessness. "You do not have because you do not ask" (James 4:2). Perhaps Peter's failure could have been averted if he had been obedient to the Lord and spent that time in the garden praying that the Lord would grant him grace to endure.

But Peter and the other disciples were so physically exhausted after a long and difficult day that they may not have even realized how much their *spiritual* strength was depleted. They certainly felt their need for physical rest more than they sensed their need for spiritual refreshment. That is why instead of renewing their spirits through prayer as Jesus repeatedly urged, they sought rest and renewal of their bodies through sleep.

He Slept Too Much

That was yet another factor in Peter's downfall. He was sound asleep when the soldiers first arrived to take Jesus. Peter was probably still shaking off his sleepy stupor when he impulsively drew his sword and struck Malchus, the high priest's servant. It was not the action of someone who was wide awake and at the peak of his sensibilities. In fact, from the moment the disciples were awakened until they made the fateful decision to forsake Jesus and flee, as little as ten minutes might have elapsed. They would have barely had time to awaken completely. Amazingly, despite all the clear warnings Jesus had given them, when the moment of truth finally arrived, they were caught completely off guard.

There is a remarkable contrast between Jesus in Gethsemane and the disciples who were there with Him. He was in agony, sorrowing heavily, wrestling in prayer—literally sweating blood in His anguish. They were sound asleep, oblivious to all that Jesus was going through, oblivious to all He had told them they would soon go through, oblivious to the approaching multitude. They were in the throes of a carnal slumber.

Even when Christ repeatedly woke them and urged them to pray, their fleshly desire for sleep was so strong that they simply could not fight it off. Consider this: If they were so weak that they could not find the strength to stay awake and pray with Christ when He was in such an obviously troubled state, whatever made them think they would have the physical stamina to stand firm with Him when their very lives were in jeopardy?

Christ's agony was more intense than anything they had ever seen before. The sight of Him sweating blood certainly should have been enough to jolt them back to consciousness and get them praying with Him. But feeling only their own physical exhaustion, they ignored their more urgent spiritual needs, and that is why they neglected prayer at the one moment they could least afford to do so.

"Now it is high time to awake out of sleep" (Romans 13:11). Neglect of prayer and too much sleep have led to the sad downfall of many saints. They were major contributing factors in Peter's failure.

He Acted Too Fast

Peter's boasting had already stoked his own sense of pride and self-sufficiency, so it is no wonder that when finally put to the test, he tried to take matters into his own hands and rely on carnal force. When the temple officers tried to apprehend Jesus, Peter "stretched out his hand and drew his sword, struck the servant of the high priest, and cut off his ear" (Matthew 26:51).

It was an impulsive and reckless thing to do. If Peter had merely followed Jesus' lead at any point that evening, he might have been spared a lot of heartache. If he had simply listened when Jesus wanted to warn him, or prayed when Jesus urged him to do so, he certainly would have been better prepared for this moment. Even now, with a large multitude of armed men threatening to arrest Jesus, common sense and basic prudence would suggest that the only right thing for the disciples to do would be to follow Jesus' lead. If Jesus wanted to resist or avoid arrest, he certainly had the ability to do so (v. 53). He had avoided arrest more than once before without resorting to violence (Luke 4:30; John 8:59).

But Peter always seemed to think he knew better, even though doing things his own way never got him anywhere but deeper into trouble.

Christ had repeatedly foretold His own arrest and death. In fact, the worst rebuke Peter ever received from his Master was the time Christ called him "Satan"—and that was because Peter insisted Jesus should not be speaking about His death. On that occasion, Christ admonished Peter for caring too much about earthly matters. The clear implication was that Jesus' death was something that would somehow advance heaven's interests. Peter could not have understood the full import of what Jesus meant at that time, but if he had merely pondered Christ's words more carefully, he might have been slower to draw his sword on this occasion.

The Lord's rebuke as He healed Malchus's ear no doubt wounded Peter's pride even more painfully than his own sword had wounded Malchus. And since Peter's courage and self-confidence were completely rooted in carnal pride, once Peter's pride was deflated, he had no reserves from which he could draw strength. Therefore he fled in fear with the other disciples.

He Followed Too Far

Peter's final step toward failure was the decision to follow Christ from a distance after fleeing from His presence. He tried to stay far enough away so that no one would suspect he was a disciple of Jesus, yet close enough to be able to see what was happening. The tactic led Peter right into the place where he would be most sorely tempted—the courtyard of the high priest—and just at the time when he was least prepared to handle such a temptation.

Peter's behavior is like that of many who fear to confess Christ openly. Because they try to avoid public identification as Christians, they are strongly inclined to act like *non*-Christians. All the temptations they face are greatly multiplied and greatly intensified. Perhaps no situation is more spiritually dangerous for a believer than the set of circumstances that arises when one attempts to conceal one's relationship with Christ. Peter discovered this the hard way.

There is nonetheless something admirable in the fact that Peter did not utterly abandon Christ, but stayed close enough to follow Him throughout the ordeal of that night. Peter's faith was weak, but it was real. His love for Christ would not permit him to abandon Christ completely. He was compelled by that love to follow his Master and keep vigil over the proceedings against Him. Both John and Peter apparently followed the arresting soldiers to the high priest's compound, where John was known to the servants and thus gained entry for himself and Peter into the courtyard (John 18:16). From there Peter was close enough to hear what was being said inside.

No more is said about John after he helped get Peter admitted into the courtyard. John apparently did not stay long at the scene. Because he was well known to the high priest's household, he might have felt the risk of being recognized was too high. He may actually have heard Peter being asked if he was one of Jesus' disciples, and if so, John probably figured he had no chance of remaining incognito in such a group, so he quietly slipped away. Scripture does not say where John went, but the fact that no more is said of him that night makes it reasonably certain that he did not stay in the high priest's courtyard very long after getting Peter admitted.

SPIRITUAL DEFEAT

Peter was admitted to the courtyard during the initial phase of the trial—while Jesus was still in Annas's house. It was almost immediately after his admission to the courtyard that he denied Christ for the first time. John writes, "The servant girl who kept the door said to Peter, 'You are not also one of this Man's disciples, are you?' He said, 'I am not'" (John 18:17). Matthew and Mark agree that this exchange took place while Peter was inside the courtyard (Matthew 26:69; Mark 14:66). He was seated (according to Luke) near the fire (Luke 22:56). Apparently the young girl who served as the high priest's doorkeeper observed Peter when he entered the courtyard and was suspicious or curious about him, so she went over by the fire for a closer look. She studied his face until she was confident of who Peter was.

A comparison of the Gospel writers' accounts suggests the dialogue that followed was more than merely a single-sentence challenge and a retort. It became a prolonged exchange, as the young woman *insisted* that Peter was one of the disciples and he vehemently denied it. John reports that the girl asked, "You are not also one of this Man's disciples, are you?" and Peter simply answered, "I am not" (John 18:17). Matthew adds more detail: "Now Peter sat outside in the courtyard. And a servant girl came to him, saying, 'You also were with Jesus of Galilee.' But he denied it before them all, saying, 'I do not know what you are saying'"(Matthew 26:69–70). Peter's denial "before them all" suggests that he made his denial loud enough to be heard by other witnesses. That is because according to Luke, the girl not only addressed her accusations to Peter, but she also attempted to expose him to the group around the fire, "This man was also with him" (Luke 22:56). Peter replied with a flat denial that he even knew Jesus: "Woman, I do not know Him" (v. 57).

Mark tells us that immediately following that exchange with the maiden, Peter left the warmth of the fire to seek a safer place away from the girl who had recognized him. "He went out on the porch, and a rooster crowed" (Mark 14:68).

Peter's conscience was probably smiting him already, and the rooster's crowing (assuming Peter noticed it) would have instantly called to mind the Lord's earlier warning. It was all coming to pass just as Jesus had said it would, and Peter may have been desperately looking for a way out. "The porch" refers to the covered gateway, a smaller forecourt leading from the inner courtyard to the street. Peter was no doubt unsettled by the fact that he had been recognized, and he might have been trying to get closer to the gate, in case he needed to make an escape. He was also obviously looking for someplace to be alone—perhaps a place where he could hide in the shadows, away from the light of the fire, and thus avoid exposure by anyone else who might recognize him.

But it was not to be. "When he had gone out to the gateway, another girl saw him and said to those who were there, 'This fellow also was with Jesus of Nazareth.' But again he denied with an oath, 'I do not know the Man!'" (Matthew 26:71–72).

Comparing the gospel accounts, we learn that several people actually took part in accusing Peter at this point. Mark writes, "The servant girl saw him again, and began to say to those who stood by, 'This is one of them'" (Mark 14:69). That suggests that the same maiden, the servant doorkeeper, again challenged Peter, this time inciting several witnesses to repeat the challenge to Peter. John makes it clear that several people accused Peter at this point: "They said to him, 'You are not also one of His disciples, are you?'" (John 18:25). And Luke says, "After a little while another saw him and said, 'You also are of them'" (Luke 22:58). Luke employs a masculine form of the pronoun "another" to suggest that the speaker he quotes was a man. Luke also makes it clear that Peter responded to a male accuser: "Man, I am not!"

So it seems a small group of people in the courtyard, following the first servant girl's lead, were now accusing Peter all at once, and his replies to their charges constituted his second denial. Again, it appears to have been a repeated and vehement denial, not a single throwaway contradiction of his accusers. To the original maiden, "he denied it again" (Mark 14:70). To one of the men who identified him as a disciple of Christ, he said, "Man, I am not" (Luke 22:58). To the whole group who pressed him to admit that he was one of the Twelve, "He denied it and said, 'I am not!'" (John 18:25). And to the second maiden, the girl mentioned by Matthew, "Again he denied with an oath, 'I do not know the Man!'" (Matthew 26:72). And thus for the second time since he entered the courtyard, he denied even knowing Jesus.

It is ironic that a couple of servant girls and a small group of household servants could elicit such an emphatic denial from Peter. Remember that only hours before this, he had insisted that he would *never* deny Christ, even if it cost him his life. In the garden, he had even been willing to use his sword against a large group of armed men. But now he was cowering and fearful because a couple of young girls identified him as a follower of Jesus.

There is nothing to suggest that the servant girls or anyone else in the courtyard would have done any harm to Peter if he had admitted to being a disciple of Christ. If that had been their intention, they would have immediately called for the officers of the court on the mere suspicion that Peter was one of Jesus' disciples. But they seem merely to have been taunting Peter. And Peter—who had so recently insisted with the utmost vehemence that he was prepared to withstand *any* assault on his loyalty—was totally blindsided by such petty harassment. He had apparently been gearing up for a frontal attack accompanied by the threat of violence against him. That is why, back in the garden, he reacted so quickly to the armed attackers—as if he was prepared to take on a whole army single-handedly. But his inability to stand strong for Christ in the face of the teasing of some young girls and household servants shows how pathetically *un*prepared Peter really was. Satan had exposed his vulnerability, and in the end no overt threat of violence or attack on his life was necessary to get him to deny his Master.

Peter's second denial, being accompanied by an oath, was an even more serious transgression than his first denial had been. An oath involves literally calling on God to be a witness to the truth of one's testimony. And an oath in that society was deemed the utmost sacred bond of truth. To compound one's lying with a false oath was to take the Lord's name in vain in the most blasphemous possible way—in effect attempting to make God a witness to a lie. Peter's sin at this point was clearly willful and deliberate. But he was caught in a sinister web of his own weaving, and there was no getting out of it now.

Peter's oath apparently had the effect of quelling the immediate accusations against him, because Luke says another hour elapsed before Peter's final denial. Peter apparently moved to a place in the courtyard where he had a clear view inside the house and could see what was happening to Jesus. Sometime during that hour, Caiaphas succeeded in eliciting the testimony from Jesus that the Sanhedrin deemed blasphemous. Mark places the beating, blindfolding, and spitting on Jesus prior to Peter's denial (Mark 14:64–66), so Peter probably witnessed the abuse Jesus suffered.

Meanwhile, the group in the courtyard may have been talking among themselves about Peter and his relationship to Jesus. They finally decided to confront him with evidence of *why* they were certain he was one of Jesus' disciples: "And a little later those who stood by came up and said to Peter, 'Surely you also are one of them, for your speech betrays you'" (Matthew 26:73). Luke says the accuser on this occasion *"Confidently* affirmed, saying, 'Surely this fellow also was with Him, for he is a Galilean'" (Luke 22:59, emphasis added).

And this time the accusers also had an eyewitness: "One of the servants of the high priest, a relative of him whose ear Peter cut off, said, 'Did I not see you in the garden with Him?'" (John 18:26).

The fact that one of Malchus's relatives recognized Peter and could place him in Gethsemane during the arrest seems to have rattled Peter severely. This time "he began to curse and swear, saying, 'I do not know the Man!'" (Matthew 26:74). The cursing and swearing were probably not the kind of coarse vulgarities and expletives we normally associate with cursing and swearing. Rather, this means that Peter pronounced a curse on himself, expressing a hope that he would die violently at God's own hand if his words were untrue. And then he swore yet another oath—calling again on God to be his witness—that he did not know Jesus. It was the strongest sort of oath it is possible to take. When a person takes such an oath and then uses it to cover a lie, it is the most reprehensible kind of lie, compounding the mere lie with an overt blasphemy, suggesting God would be witness to a lie—and calling the judgment of God down on one's own head in the process. But by this time Peter seems to have lost all sense of the Lord's true presence. He was now so desperate to confirm his own lie that he threw off all restraint.

"Immediately, while he was still speaking, the rooster crowed" (Luke 22:60). This was the second rooster-crowing, according to Mark, who is the only one of the gospel writers to record that Jesus said, "Before the rooster crows *twice,* you will deny Me three times" (Mark 14:72, emphasis added; cf. v. 30). The other writers employ a kind of ellipsis, mentioning only the *fact* of the rooster-crowing. Mark alone saw fit to specify how many times the rooster crowed. He noted this detail apparently to underscore how precisely Jesus had predicted Peter's failure. Mark no doubt learned of the incident from Peter himself. (Mark's gospel was even referred to in the early church as "the memoirs of Peter," because Peter was obviously the primary human source of the unique details Mark recorded.) Peter himself might have wished to emphasize that the rooster crowed twice, because it showed how patient the Lord had been with him, giving him so many warning signals and tokens of His grace—even while Peter persisted in a course of sinful denial.

It was precisely at the moment of the second rooster-crowing that (according to Luke) "The Lord turned and looked at Peter. And Peter remembered the word of the Lord, how He had said to him, 'Before the rooster crows, you will deny Me three times'" (Luke 22:61). The Lord must have been positioned precisely where he could turn and look out an open window and into Peter's eyes. His already battered face, so recently beaten and spat upon by evil men, turned in that instant toward Peter, and His loving but all-knowing eyes met Peter's eyes and looked into his very soul. The verb Luke employs is *emblepo,* which describes a fixed look, almost like a stare. It wasn't an accusing glare, but a tender, piercing look that broke Peter's heart.

REPENTANCE

As Jesus made eye contact with Peter, "Peter remembered. . . . So he went out and wept bitterly" (Matthew 26:75). Peter's true character is seen not in his denial of Christ, but in his repentance. Notice, first of all, how quickly he repented. Instantly, when the rooster crowed and Christ looked at Peter, Peter's conscience was smitten. He left the high priest's compound and went somewhere alone to weep bitterly.

Where Peter went is not mentioned. It may have been just outside Caiaphas's courtyard, in one of the alleyways nearby. Or he may have gone back to Gethsemane, that familiar place that had become Jesus' customary evening retreat with His disciples—back to the place where he ought to have been weeping and praying hours before. In any case, Peter did not defer his repentance until a more convenient day. He immediately recalled Jesus' words and the tender warning he had so callously spurned only hours earlier, and he inwardly confessed his own wrong and was overwhelmed with sorrow because of it.

Tears of repentance can in no way atone for sins. (Only Jesus' death can do that.) But genuine sorrow is nonetheless an important sign of true repentance, signifying that a change of mind and heart have truly taken place.

Not *all* sorrow signifies true repentance, however. "Godly sorrow produces repentance leading to salvation, not to be regretted; but the sorrow of the world produces death" (2 Corinthians 7:10). As we shall shortly see, Judas would express sorrow too. According to Matthew 27:3–5, Judas was remorseful over what he had done and tried to return the blood money to the ruling priests. His guilt over what he had done finally even motivated him to go out and kill himself. But that kind of sorrow is a worldly sorrow that only leads to death. It may involve sincere remorse over the *consequences* of one's sin— regret over the loss of prestige or friends or influence. But it reflects no true change of heart, and thus no true grief over the sin itself.

Peter's sorrow was of a different sort. "He wept bitterly" (Matthew 26:75). It was the deepest possible sorrow of heart—mingled with shame over his sinful behavior, hatred of the sin itself, and a desperate longing to be restored to a right relationship with Christ.

Peter might have thought all hope of reconciliation with Christ was gone. After all, he had heard Jesus teach that whoever denied Him before men He would deny before the Father (Matthew 10:33). Possibly fearing he had forfeited his relationship with Christ forever, and still reeling from a deep sense of sorrow over his own sin, Peter did not seem to regain his full confidence even when he learned that Christ had risen from the dead. From Peter's perspective, even the triumph of the resurrection seemed somewhat dimmed by the bitter memory of his failure.

In fact, shortly after the resurrection, Peter decided to return to his previous vocation as a fisherman, taking several other disciples with him (cf. John 21:3). It was then that Christ made a special appearance to them and questioned Peter about his love for Him. Three times Peter had denied Christ. Three times Jesus asked Peter about his love. And three times Peter affirmed that he still loved Him (John 21:15–17). In the process, Christ recommissioned him for ministry, proving that even such a serious sin is forgivable when the sinner's repentance is genuine.

And Peter's repentance was certainly genuine. He never again denied Christ. As a matter of fact, for the remainder of his life, Peter distinguished himself for his bold proclamation of Christ, even in the most hostile situations. A mere fifty days after that awful night of Peter's denial, Peter would stand before thousands in Jerusalem at the feast of Pentecost, and he would deliver one of the most bold and forceful sermons ever preached. Starting with that great triumph at Pentecost, Peter would be used of the Lord to point untold numbers of people to Christ (see Acts 2–12).

The marvelous way Peter was forgiven and restored by Christ is proof of the thoroughness of Peter's repentance. He never forgot the bitterness of his denial, and thus he never again returned to that sin. According to one legend that was widely circulated in the early church, as long as Peter lived, the sound of a rooster crowing always caused him to weep.

What is most notable about the whole episode, however, is the depth of the grace and the wonder of forgiveness that can restore such a fallen saint to such an extraordinary position of usefulness. Again we are reminded that the ignominy and the scandal of Peter's sin are not where Scripture places the stress. Instead, this whole episode is recounted in all four gospels mainly to highlight the grace that was subsequently shown to Peter. It is one of the most graphic proofs of the wonderful, unassailable security with which all who belong to Christ are kept by Him (cf. John 6:37–40).

Hours before Peter's denial, Christ had prayed, "Those whom You gave Me I have kept; and none of them is lost except the son of perdition, that the Scripture might be fulfilled" (John 17:12). Jesus knew Peter would stumble, but He also knew that Peter would repent and be restored after his failure—just as He knew Judas's treachery grew out of a final, irremediable rejection of the truth. Both Peter's repentance and Judas's apostasy were in perfect accord with the plan and purposes of God.

Peter truly belonged to Christ, and therefore Christ Himself kept Peter from stumbling so badly that he would be destroyed. Peter later cited the keeping power of God as an encouragement to other Christians being threatened with persecution. He wrote,

> Blessed be the God and Father of our Lord Jesus Christ, who according to His abundant mercy has begotten us again to a living hope through the resurrection of Jesus Christ from the dead, to an inheritance incorruptible and undefiled and that does not fade away, reserved in heaven for you, who are *kept by the power of God* through

faith for salvation ready to be revealed in the last time. In this you greatly rejoice, though now for a little while, if need be, you have been grieved by various trials, that the genuineness of your faith, being much more precious than gold that perishes, though it is tested by fire, may be found to praise, honor, and glory at the revelation of Jesus Christ. (1 Peter 1:3–7, emphasis added)

Peter undoubtedly remembered his own experience as he penned that paragraph. He knew better than anyone did how wonderful it is to be kept by God. He knew full well that his security was not the fruit of his own faithfulness—but he had been kept in the faith by God's grace even when his own fleshly tendency was to be *un*faithful and abandon Christ. It was God who graciously drew him back, and it was God who kept his faith from failing even in the midst of his trials. Peter could take no credit whatsoever for having avoided ultimate failure.

Notice that Peter did not tell believers they must somehow secure themselves in Christ. He did not suggest that their security was somehow dependent on their own faithfulness. He did not give them a pep talk or try to drum up their courage. He remembered too well the folly of his own self-sufficiency and self-reliance.

Instead, he pointed them to the One who was truly able to keep them from falling, and to present them faultless before His throne (cf. Jude 25). It was the Lord who kept Peter, and it the Lord who ensures every believer's ultimate security. Our own fleshly tendencies may fill us with doubt and fear and uncertainty—and well they should. But it is to His faithfulness that we should turn for strength and encouragement, for "[Even when] we are faithless, He remains faithful; He cannot deny Himself" (2 Timothy 2:13).

8

When morning came, all the chief priests and elders of the people plotted against Jesus to put Him to death.

—MATTHEW 27:1

8

❧ Crucifixion Morning

PETER'S FINAL DENIAL OF CHRIST, marked by the second rooster-crowing, occurred sometime in the very early hours of the morning—probably an hour or two before dawn broke on the eastern horizon. When Peter left the scene, the proceedings inside Caiaphas's house were probably beginning to wind down. The hour was extremely late. The Sanhedrin had already agreed on a guilty verdict, and the sentence of death had also been passed. The only remaining problems they had to face were how to legitimize the trial, and how best to implement the penalty.

THE STRATEGIZING OF THE SANHEDRIN

The Sanhedrin needed a careful strategy for pursuing their case against Jesus. A few years prior to this, Rome had rescinded the Jewish leaders' right to carry out the death penalty on their own (cf. John 18:31). All capital punishment had to be approved and implemented by Roman authorities. The only exception was if a Gentile defiled the temple by traversing beyond the court of the

Gentiles, he could be stoned on the spot. Sometimes overzealous Jews would also stone people caught in the act of a capital crime. (The men in John 8:3–11, for example, wanted to stone the woman they had caught in the act of adultery.) The history of that era reveals that sometimes for the sake of political expediency Rome would turn a blind eye to such stonings—especially when they were carried out by people at the grass roots level (cf. Acts 7:54–60). But such tolerance would not have been extended to official verdicts rendered by the Sanhedrin. As the only Jewish court recognized and authorized by Rome, they were expected to abide by Roman policies limiting their power.

Furthermore, the authority of the Sanhedrin was confined to religious matters, and therefore relatively few of the cases they heard involved capital crimes. In extreme cases they might be able to gain Roman approval for enacting the death penalty against a particularly unruly blasphemer. But obviously the Romans (who were committed to their own mythical brand of polytheism) were not eager to incite Jewish enthusiasm for having heretics put to death.

If the Sanhedrin intended to ask Rome to execute the death penalty against Jesus, they would have to present the case against Him in a compelling way. The believability of their case against Jesus was severely compromised by the way the trial had been conducted so quickly and under cover of darkness. That may be why during the early hours of the morning (probably around 3:00 or 4:00 A.M.), the council decided to adjourn until later that morning. No doubt all were exhausted anyway. The recess would give council members time for a couple of hours' sleep, and the court could be officially reconvened in the daylight hours to render a formal verdict, in keeping with the required procedure for such cases. This way if anyone questioned the justice of the way the Sanhedrin had tried Christ, they could claim that their final verdict had been reached in full daylight.

They wasted no time. Luke reports that the Sanhedrin reconvened their council and brought Jesus in for their final hearing of His case "as soon as it was day" (Luke 22:66). Matthew describes the same meeting: "When morning came, all the chief priests and elders of the people plotted against Jesus to put Him to death" (Matthew 27:1).

Christ had been kept under guard all night, possibly in a dungeon at Caiaphas's house. At the site in Jerusalem traditionally believed to be the location of Caiaphas's house, there is a small, ancient stone dungeon with an opening just large enough for one person to be lowered into the dungeon. After His trial ended, Christ may have been confined in such a prison for the remainder of the night, or He may have been held in a room in Caiaphas's house under armed guard. In either case, when morning came, He was bound again (His hands tied tightly behind His back in the customary manner of binding a criminal) and brought once more before the Sanhedrin, so that they could make their verdict official, and determine how to implement their sentence of death against Him.

The council subjected Christ once more to the same line of questioning Caiaphas had used the night before. Luke describes the hearing:

> As soon as it was day, the elders of the people, both chief priests and scribes, came together and led Him into their council, saying, "If You are the Christ, tell us." But He said to them, "If I tell you, you will by no means believe. And if I also ask you, you will by no means answer Me or let Me go. Hereafter the Son of Man will sit on the right hand of the power of God." Then they all said, "Are You then the Son of God?" So He said to them, "You rightly say that I am." And they said, "What further testimony do we need? For we have heard it ourselves from His own mouth."
> (Luke 22:66–71)

They wanted Jesus to state plainly whether He was the Messiah. Having solicited many witnesses against Him, they were nonetheless unable to prove that He had ever publicly declared (in so many words) that He was the Christ. Indeed He was the Christ, but this was not a claim He overtly made for Himself in public settings. That is why when Peter said, "You are the Christ, the Son of the living God," Jesus replied, "Blessed are you, Simon Bar-Jonah, for flesh and blood has not revealed this to you, but My Father who is in heaven" (Matthew 16:16–17). And then He commanded the disciples not to tell anyone that He was the Messiah (v. 20).

People who heard Jesus teach had varying opinions about who He was. He asked the disciples, "Who do men say that I, the Son of Man, am?" The reply shows what a diverse array of opinions were being set forth about His true identity: "Some say John the Baptist, some Elijah, and others Jeremiah or one of the prophets" (vv. 13–14).

There was such a wide difference of opinion about who He was because He had never explicitly stated in His public teaching that He was the Messiah. He had implied that He was fulfilling prophecies that referred to the Messiah (Luke 4:18–21). He had privately told individuals that He was the Messiah (John 4:25–26). He had said the Old Testament Scriptures pointed to Him (John 5:39). It was certainly well known that His closest followers believed He was the Messiah. His triumphal entry into Jerusalem less than a week before His arrest revealed how widespread that belief was. But the Sanhedrin was determined to have Him state from His own lips for the record whether He claimed to be the Messiah.

Jesus' reply exposed the council's prejudice. If He claimed to be the Messiah, they would not believe the claim, nor would they give any serious consideration to any proofs He might bring forth. They had already seen and heard about many of the amazing proofs of His divine power. In fact, one of His greatest miracles—the raising of Lazarus—was what finally sealed their determination to kill Him (John 11:53).

Furthermore, as He pointed out, *He* had already questioned *them* about His Messianic credentials, and they had refused to answer (cf. Luke 20:3–7, 41–44). If they could not answer the evidence that showed He was the Messiah, they ought to let Him go. But it was quite clear that they had no intention of doing either. Jesus was being railroaded; this was no legitimate trial.

But even though they did not now believe His claims, He solemnly assured them that the time would come when the Son of Man would sit on the right hand of the power of God. He was implying that the tables would one day be turned and He would sit in judgment of them.

His reply didn't quite give them what they wanted, however, so they pressed further: "Are You then the Son of God?" This time He replied simply, "You rightly say that I am" (Luke 22:70).

That was just what they wanted. Now they had Him on record, in broad daylight, claiming to be the Son of God. As He had just pointed out, whether that claim was true or not made no difference whatsoever to them. Though He had given ample evidence throughout His ministry to substantiate the claim—although some of these men had even seen that evidence with their own eyes—they were not the least bit interested in either establishing or disproving the validity of His claim; all they wanted to do now was get Him on the cross as quickly as possible. In the end, it meant they crucified Him for telling the truth.

As soon as Jesus claimed to be the Son of God, the trial was immediately brought to a close. "What further testimony do we need?" (v. 71). As had happened the night before, He was offered no opportunity to call witnesses in His defense. None of the evidence establishing the veracity of His claim was permitted. Evidence was irrelevant as far as these men were concerned. They had actually reached their guilty verdict beforehand. Christ's testimony gave them the appearance of legitimacy they needed. As far as they were concerned, all "further testimony" would be superfluous and counterproductive. They now were eager to move ahead with the execution of their sentence.

The decision was made immediately to take Jesus to Pontius Pilate to get Roman permission to have Him put to death—preferably by Roman executioners. "They led Him away and delivered Him to Pontius Pilate the governor" (Matthew 27:2).

THE SUICIDE OF JUDAS

At this point in Matthew's gospel he interrupts his account of Jesus' trials to recount Judas's earthly demise. It may well be that this part of the story properly fits here chronologically. Or it may be that Matthew placed it here in order to make a stark contrast between the vile iniquity represented by Judas and the utter purity represented by Jesus. In either case, coming at this point, it emphasizes the utter injustice of Jesus' death, as seen in the fact that even the one who betrayed Him was so smitten in conscience as to be quite literally unable to live with himself.

Matthew writes,

> Then Judas, His betrayer, seeing that He had been condemned, was remorseful and brought back the thirty pieces of silver to the chief priests and elders, saying, "I have sinned by betraying innocent blood." And they said, "What is that to us? You see to it!" Then he threw down the pieces of silver in the temple and departed, and went and hanged himself. (Matthew 27:3–5)

Matthew's language supports the idea that this event is included at this point because it fits here chronologically: *"Then* Judas . . .

seeing that He had been condemned" (v. 3). We are not told where Judas was while Jesus was on trial. It seems unlikely that he would have had an active part in the trial. His testimony would have been compromised and probably thought inadmissible because of his status as a turncoat and traitor. As is obvious from events that follow, even Judas's fellow conspirators had little use for him once his act of betrayal was complete. Judas immediately became an utter outcast, despised by all for his treacherous behavior.

Yet Judas had an obvious interest in the outcome of the trial. Like Peter, he seems to have followed from a distance. At the very least, it appears he was present at the conclusion of the Sanhedrin's final daylight hearing, because Matthew says he *saw* that Christ had been condemned. Perhaps as Judas saw Jesus bound and led away to Pilate, the full enormity of his sin finally dawned on him. The sight of Jesus being so mistreated because of his betrayal was more than even Judas could handle. At that moment, Judas may have begun to realize for the first time the magnitude of his own sinful foolishness. He had sold the Son of God for a handful of money. He had squandered the incredible opportunity of close fellowship and discipleship with God incarnate that had been his as one of the inner circle of twelve. Only eleven other men in all history have enjoyed that kind of intimate, personal, face-to-face relationship with God the Son. No one else has ever been exposed to so much truth from the lips of the Lord and rejected it all. No one else was ever privileged to witness the Lord's example firsthand and close-up for so long—and yet spurned Him anyway.

History is full of villains who *appear* more despicable than Judas Iscariot. Compare Judas with someone who has perpetrated genocide or lived a life of wanton, scandalous evil, and Judas might not appear so bad. But the truth is that no one could ever be more evil than he was. No one ever sinned against so much light and so much privilege. No one ever betrayed so innocent a victim. No one ever maintained such a hard heart for so long in the presence of so much compassionate goodness. Remember, Judas had received all the same tokens of divine loving-kindness from Christ as the other disciples in his three years with the Master.

But all those privileges had never impacted Judas's heart in the least. For three years he resisted and rejected all the truth he heard from Jesus. He hardened his heart against it, and he secretly grew to despise the sinless Son of God. Yet throughout those years he was such an expert in the art of hypocrisy that he managed to conceal his true character from everyone except Jesus. And in the end, he happily sold all his spiritual advantages—including Christ Himself—to the highest bidder. The evil of his heart defies comprehension.

No wonder Jesus called him a devil (John 6:70). No wonder Satan had such easy access to Judas's heart (John 13:27; Luke 22:3). No more sordid soul ever walked the face of the earth.

But even Judas could not escape the horrifying pain of his own guilt. The time finally came when even a heart so severely hardened and a conscience so badly seared could not cushion his soul from the sense of guilt he will bear throughout eternity.

As soon as Judas saw Jesus bound and led away, he was smitten with regret. It was not true repentance, but merely remorse. (Though the King James Version says Judas "repented himself," the word used is not the normal Greek word for repentance, *metanoeō*, but another word that merely signifies deep regret, *metamelomai*.) Judas was beginning to realize the bitter consequences of sin, and he hated those consequences; but he never reached the point where he hated the sin itself.

Why was Judas suddenly filled with regret when he saw that Jesus had been condemned? He may have thought when he betrayed Him that Jesus would escape arrest as He had done repeatedly before. Or perhaps Judas assumed Jesus would be able to clear Himself of any charges brought against Him. After all, He was truly innocent of any wrongdoing. And Judas had never seen Christ *fail* in any circumstances. Judas may have actually hoped Jesus would escape or be vindicated. It would be the perfect scenario. Judas would still have his thirty pieces of silver. Jesus would be no worse off for the experience. The hypocritical priests would simply be out thirty pieces of silver. Using that sort of rationale, Judas may have convinced himself that his betrayal of Jesus was no great thing and would have no serious or lasting consequences—especially if Jesus really was the true Messiah.

But now the sight of Christ condemned caused him to see for the first time the true enormity of his guilt. And it was more than he could bear.

Judas desperately wanted to escape the consequences of what he had done. Notice what he did in his effort to escape his guilt. By human standards, these might seem rather impressive evidences of a kind of repentance. *First, he offered restitution.* He took the thirty pieces of silver back to the Sanhedrin and futilely begged them to take it back. He may have done this while they were still assembled at the end of Jesus' final hearing, immediately after Christ had been led away to Pilate. The money was all Judas had wanted before; now he was suddenly desperate to get rid of it, because it was the physical reminder of the guilt that pained him so much. It had suddenly become like a live coal in his hands. *Second, he offered a confession.* Judas verbally confessed his guilt. He acknowledged that he had sinned; he also affirmed Jesus' innocence. He made no excuses for his action, but freely admitted his wrong.

Those measures at first glance may appear to have taken him a long way toward repentance, but he still fell far short. It's true that he confessed that he had sinned, but he did not confess to God and seek true forgiveness. He didn't come like the Prodigal Son to the

One he had sinned against. There was evidently no more love for Christ in his heart when he brought the money back to the Sanhedrin than when they gave him the money in the first place. The only thing that had changed was that he now felt the repercussions of his sin powerfully, and he wanted no part of his sin's *consequences*. Like so many who profess repentance today, Judas mostly just wanted to get rid of the pain his guilt caused him. The constant torment of his own conscience pangs was too much for him, and he wanted relief.

Sin never truly satisfies. There are momentary pleasures in sin (cf. Hebrews 11:25), but they invariably give way to sorrow and misery and pain. In a moment of pleasure seeking motivated by his love of money, Judas had bartered away any opportunity of real joy or satisfaction forever. Paul wrote, "The love of money is a root of all kinds of evil, for which some have strayed from the faith in their greediness, and pierced themselves through with many sorrows" (1 Timothy 6:10). Judas is the prototype of what Paul was describing. No one ever pierced himself through with more sorrow—and all for the foolish love of money.

Judas would receive no sympathy or support from his fellow conspirators. Their response to his confession was in effect sheer mockery: "And they said, 'What is that to us? You see to it!'" (Matthew 27:4). They were too preoccupied with other things to deal with Judas at the moment. They had to get Jesus on the cross. The callousness of their reply is astonishing. Judas plainly admitted to them that he had betrayed innocent blood. The fact that this meant nothing to them reveals how purely evil their intentions were from the very beginning. They were going to crucify Jesus with the full knowledge of His innocence.

Judas could not get them to take the money back, so he threw it into the temple and left. This may mean that he threw the money inside the holy place, where only priests could go, thus *forcing* the priests to retrieve the money themselves. It was a final act of spite, designed to make them own the silver coins that had become the token of Judas's guilt.

Deuteronomy 27:25 says, "Cursed is the one who takes a bribe to slay an innocent person." Judas must have superstitiously associated the physical coins themselves with the curse, and he may have hoped to rid himself of the curse by ridding himself of the money. At the very least, he wanted to bring the same curse on his fellow conspirators. That explains this little game of hot potato he was playing with the money. By throwing the money and leaving quickly, he left them no choice but to take the money back.

Judas, utterly friendless, hopeless, and disconsolate under the weight of his own guilt, then sealed his self-destruction forever with an act of suicide.

Perhaps Judas thought by killing himself he could finally get relief from his guilt. The opposite is true. By killing himself he bound himself to his guilt forever. Judas of all people ought to have known this, for he had repeatedly heard Jesus teach about hell—how it is a place of eternal torment, unquenchable fire, and weeping and gnashing of teeth that goes on day and night forever (Matthew 8:12; 13:42, 50; 22:13; 24:51; 25:30; Luke 13:28; Mark 9:43–48). In hell the pain of guilt and conscience pangs are eternally intensified—eating away at the soul like a worm that never is satisfied and never dies.

The full circumstances of Judas's suicide may be gleaned by comparing Matthew's account with Acts 1, where Luke records the apostle Peter's words about Judas, and then adds this parenthetical comment: "Now this man purchased a field with the wages of iniquity; and falling headlong, he burst open in the middle and all his entrails gushed out. And it became known to all those dwelling in

Jerusalem; so that field is called in their own language, *Akel Dama,* that is, Field of Blood" (Acts 1:18–19).

Combining Luke's and Matthew's accounts, we can piece together what happened. Judas hanged himself on a weak branch of a tree— perhaps a limb overhanging a cliff or some sharp, jagged rocks in the potter's field. The limb must have broken, and Judas fell head-long onto the rocks, causing the horrible mutilation to his body Luke describes in the Acts 1 passage.

THE SANCTIMONY OF THE TEMPLE AUTHORITIES

The chief priests seemed to share Judas's superstitious attitude to-ward the blood money. Although Judas had managed to force them to be responsible for it, they had no desire to possess the money, nor were they willing to put it back into in the temple treasury. Matthew writes,

> The chief priests took the silver pieces and said, "It is not lawful to put them into the treasury, because they are the price of blood." And they consulted together and bought with them the potter's field, to bury strangers in. Therefore that field has been called the Field of Blood to this day. Then was fulfilled what was spoken by Jeremiah the prophet, saying, "And they took the thirty pieces of silver, the value of Him who was priced, whom they of the children of Israel priced, and gave them for the potter's field, as the LORD directed me." (Matthew 27:6–10)

Matthew's reference to Jeremiah is actually an allusion to Zechariah 11:12–13: "So they weighed out for my wages thirty pieces of silver. And the LORD said to me, 'Throw it to the potter'—that princely price they set on me. So I took the thirty pieces of silver and threw them into the house of the LORD for the potter." Zechariah thus prefigured Judas's actions with uncanny accuracy. (Matthew's attribution to "Jeremiah" reflects the common way the Hebrew canon was divided into three sections: law, writings, and prophets. Just as the poetic writings were sometimes referred to collectively as "the psalms" after the first book in that part of the canon—cf. Luke 24:44—the prophetic writings were sometimes called "Jeremiah," after the first book in the prophetic part of the Hebrew canon.)

Matthew and Luke both mention that the field had become well known as "the Field of Blood." It was evidently a familiar place by the time the gospels were written, about thirty years after the crucifixion.

On the day Judas died there, however, it was known as "the potter's field." It was probably a vacant lot attached to a potter's business—perhaps a place where clay had once been found in abundance, but the clay supply had been depleted so that the property was no longer useful to the potter. The mining of clay would have severely disfigured and devalued the property, so that thirty pieces of silver would certainly have been plenty to make the purchase.

Although Luke seems to suggest that Judas himself bought the field, he undoubtedly meant nothing more than that it was purchased with Judas's money. It is obvious from Matthew's account that the temple authorities are the ones who actually made the purchase—and they probably bought the field after Judas had died in it. They then converted the property into a cemetery for "strangers"—most likely Gentiles or outcasts.

The transaction had the appearance of an act of charity, but in reality it was rife with the grossest hypocrisy. Up to this point in their dealings with Jesus, the Sanhedrin had shown little concern for legal propriety. They had violated virtually every principle of justice in order to obtain a guilty verdict against Jesus. They had taken money from the temple treasury in order to bribe Judas to betray his Master. But on this question of whether they could place the bribe money back into the temple treasury, they suddenly began to show scruples. (Possibly this was because of a superstition like Judas's, which seemed to associate the curse of Deuteronomy 27:25 with the actual silver coins—rather than understanding that the deed of betrayal itself is the reason for the curse.)

The priests condemned themselves when they admitted that the silver pieces were "blood money." They were virtually confessing that the money was (in the words of Deuteronomy 27:25) "a bribe to slay an innocent person." In stark contrast to Judas, these men seemed to feel no pangs of conscience whatsoever for the evil deed they were doing. "What is that to us?" they mockingly replied to Judas.

Their only concern was the outward appearance of things. This was the consistent error of most of the scribes, Pharisees, Sadducees, and other Jewish religious leaders of Jesus' day. They had perfected external obedience to the law. They had mastered the art of appearing holy in other men's eyes. Their clothing, their actions, and their religious rituals were all aimed at the *appearance* of holiness. But they were neglecting weightier matters—especially true, inward righteousness. They were hypocrites. Jesus rebuked them for cleaning the outside of their cups and leaving all the rottenness on the inside. He likened them to whitewashed tombs, bright and clean-looking on the outside, but full of death and defilement on the inside:

Woe to you, scribes and Pharisees, hypocrites! For you cleanse the outside of the cup and dish, but inside they are full of extortion and self-indulgence. Blind Pharisee, first cleanse the inside of the cup and dish, that the outside of them may be clean also. Woe to you, scribes and Pharisees, hypocrites! For you are like whitewashed tombs which indeed appear beautiful outwardly, but inside are full of dead men's bones and all uncleanness. Even so you also outwardly appear righteous to men, but inside you are full of hypocrisy and lawlessness. (Matthew 23:25–28)

Jesus had consistently taught on this theme from the beginning of His public ministry. It was the central message of His Sermon on the Mount—where He taught that the real significance of God's moral law pertains to the heart, not external matters like clothing or ritual or public behavior (Matthew 6).

The members of the Sanhedrin who condemned Christ epitomized the gross hypocrisy He had always opposed. They sanctimoniously refused to put blood money into the temple treasury in broad daylight, but they had no compunctions about secretly *paying* blood money from the treasury to Judas. They weren't concerned about their own awful guilt; they were concerned only about how they appeared to others. They had no time to consider Jesus' innocence ("What is that to us?")—they were too busy trying to make it appear as if He deserved death. As long as they could cloak their evil conspiracy with an illusion of legitimacy, they were perfectly content to pursue their course of sin. They would do everything in their power to make Jesus appear guilty and themselves appear righteous—even though they knew very well that, in reality, the opposite was true.

Now they were off to try to enlist the Romans in the conspiracy to murder Jesus.

9

The governor answered and said to them, "Which of the two do you want me to release to you?" They said, "Barrabas!" Pilate said to them, "What then shall I do with Jesus who is called Christ?" They all said to him, "Let Him be crucified!"

—MATTHEW 27:21–22

9

 What Shall I Do with Jesus?

IMMEDIATELY AFTER the early-morning hearing in which the Sanhedrin reaffirmed their death sentence against Jesus, they bound Him and marched Him off to the Roman governor of Judea, Pontius Pilate (Matthew 27:2).

All criminal penalties in Judea were subject to Pilate's ultimate approval or veto (either directly or through courts that operated under his oversight). The Sanhedrin constituted a religious court, not a civil one. Their jurisdiction covered matters directly pertaining to the Jewish religion. They had no authority to put anyone to death without prior Roman approval (John 18:31)—even in cases where Old Testament law prescribed death. That meant many Old Testament moral and religious standards could not be enforced with biblical penalties. The Romans rarely approved the death penalty in cases of adultery, homosexuality, blasphemy, false prophecy—or other moral or religious transgressions.

That policy was widely resented as a Roman intrusion into the Jewish religion—and an affront to the law of God. It was one of the main points of constant friction between the Sanhedrin and the Roman government. Nonetheless, the members of the Sanhedrin on this occasion were eager to get Roman consent to Jesus' death, because that would help legitimize what they were doing. Perhaps they somehow thought if they could dupe the Roman government into killing Jesus, His blood would not be on their hands.

They originally found Pilate unwilling to add his imprimatur to their conspiracy, but in the end Pilate decided it was politically expedient for him to kill Jesus. Pilate's political ambitions thus took precedence over whatever moral convictions he might have had, and he was the one who finally signed the death warrant to murder Jesus.

Within eighteen hours after His arrest, Jesus was subjected to two trials, each with three phases. In His trial before the Sanhedrin, there had been three hearings—one before Annas, one before the Sanhedrin at night with Caiaphas presiding, and one in the early morning, where the formal verdict was finalized. The Roman trial would also have three phases, as Christ is first brought to Pilate; then sent to Herod; then brought before Pilate once more.

Pilate's Jerusalem residence was known as the Praetorium. It was more than just his residence; it also housed the judgment hall from which he adjudicated all cases brought before him. Its location is disputed, but it was situated either next to Herod's palace, or perhaps more likely, adjacent to the Antonia fortress, the nerve center of Roman military power in Jerusalem, directly north of the temple compound. Pilate's *permanent* residence was actually in Caesarea, a town west of Jerusalem on Israel's Mediterranean coast, but he came to Jerusalem during the Jewish feasts, and thus he was in town for the Passover.

THE CROWD'S ACCUSATION

It was still very early in the morning on Friday—probably before 5:00—when the Sanhedrin arrived at the Praetorium with Jesus in shackles. Pilate could not have known beforehand of their coming, and he probably had to be awakened to meet with them at such an hour.

John 18:28–29 sets the scene: "They led Jesus from Caiaphas to the Praetorium, and it was early morning. But they themselves did not go into the Praetorium, lest they should be defiled, but that they might eat the Passover. Pilate then went out to them"—probably addressing them from a portico or balcony of the mansion.

As we saw in chapter 2, a difference in how days were reckoned made it possible for Passover to be celebrated over a two-day period. Galilean Jews reckoned their days from sunrise to sunrise, and so their Passover (14 Nisan) fell on Thursday. That is why Jesus and the disciples had already eaten the Passover meal the preceding evening. But in Judea, where days were counted by the Sadducees' method—from sundown to sundown—14 Nisan was Friday. So the Passover meal would not be eaten by most Judean Jews until later that evening. The Sanhedrin therefore would not enter Pilate's residence, because rabbinical tradition (not Scripture) taught that if they entered the home of a Gentile, they would be ceremonially defiled and unable to partake of the Passover feast. Therefore they insisted on meeting Pilate outside.

The melodrama of their refusing to enter the Praetorium actually worked in favor of the Sanhedrin's purpose, which was the political intimidation of Pilate. They had deliberately come en masse (cf. Luke 23:1) and at such an early hour on a feast day in order to lend a sense of the utmost urgency to their plea. Here was a case that clearly could not wait. The early-morning hour, the Sanhedrin's insistence on dealing with this case before they celebrated their feast, and the ploy of bringing Pilate out to meet them on their own ground all worked to underscore in Pilate's mind that this was an extremely volatile and urgent situation. The Sanhedrin no doubt hoped Pilate would simply do whatever they told him, because it was obviously advantageous for him to keep the ruling priests happy during the feast days, with so many Jewish pilgrims in town.

But Pilate was unwilling to be made their puppet so easily. He would not approve their sentence against Jesus without first hearing formal charges. So he asked them, "What accusation do you bring against this Man?" (John 18:29).

Their reply was deliberately evasive. They had actually convicted Jesus on charges of blasphemy, but they knew such a charge alone would normally be insufficient to elicit Pilate's approval for an execution. So "they answered and said to him, 'If He were not an evildoer, we would not have delivered Him up to you'" (v. 30).

The arrogance of the reply is astonishing. The Sanhedrin was in effect demanding that Pilate take Jesus and execute Him without asking any questions about what He had been accused of or why He was condemned. They pretended Pilate was impugning their integrity by trying to investigate the charges against Jesus, but the fact is that Pilate's question was one of the few proper legal procedures that was followed in all the hearings Jesus was subjected to. Pilate was refusing to hear Jesus' case until he heard the indictment.

The Sanhedrin's brash reply evidently had the desired effect on Pilate, however, because "Then Pilate said to them, 'You take Him and judge Him according to your law'" (v. 31). In effect, he gave them approval to do with Jesus whatever their law demanded. In all likelihood, Pilate assumed they would eagerly accept his nod of approval and immediately take Jesus out and stone Him. He was in essence telling the Sanhedrin that if they wanted to put Jesus to death for His supposed crimes against Judaism, Rome would turn a blind eye to the deed this time. Pilate obviously had no desire to rile the Sanhedrin on this occasion.

But the Sanhedrin was not satisfied with Pilate's approval to stone Jesus themselves. They wanted a Roman execution. This was their plan for a number of reasons. Like Pilate, they were fearful of the people's opinions (Matthew 26:5). All along, the Sanhedrin had been eager to avoid responsibility for their actions, and stoning Him by their own hands would ultimately make it impossible for them to do so. Turning Jesus over to the Romans made their plot so much more tidy. Furthermore, according to a =tradition similar to the one that forbade them to partake of the feast after entering a Gentile's house, they would have been defiled if they had stoned Jesus before eating the Passover. And now that their plot against Him was moving ahead so quickly, they had apparently decided that they did not want to delay the execution until after Passover (cf. Matthew 26:5). So they were determined to get Pilate to do the deed for them. Once they saw how easily intimidated he was, their determination only intensified.

So they told Pilate, "It is not lawful for us to put anyone to death" (John 18:31). They reminded Pilate of the very restriction they resented so much. In this case, they were determined to use it to their advantage, by intimidating Pilate further until he agreed to have Jesus put to death by Roman hands.

All of this, again, perfectly fulfilled the plan of God. By insisting on a Roman execution, the Sanhedrin was unwittingly ensuring "that the saying of Jesus might be fulfilled which He spoke, signifying by what death He would die" (v. 32). Jesus had once told his disciples, "Behold, we are going up to Jerusalem, and the Son of Man will be betrayed to the chief priests and to the scribes; and they will condemn Him to death, and deliver Him to the Gentiles to mock and to scourge and to crucify" (Matthew 20:18–19). He had many times spoken of dying on a cross—a Roman instrument of execution. By handing Jesus over for execution to the Romans, the Sanhedrin brought about the fulfillment of Jesus' own words.

But Pilate insisted on hearing an indictment against Jesus, so if the Sanhedrin wanted Pilate to execute Him, they now needed more substantial charges against Him. They would have to accuse Him of crimes that would stimulate a Roman's appetite for justice more than the accusation of blasphemy would. Therefore they quickly fabricated new charges of sedition against Him. Luke writes, "They began to accuse Him, saying, 'We found this fellow perverting the nation, and forbidding to pay taxes to Caesar, saying that He Himself is Christ, a King'" (Luke 23:2). In other words, they portrayed Him to Pilate as an insurrectionist who had deliberately stirred the people against Roman taxation and made Himself out to be a king.

None of those things were true, of course—and Pilate clearly knew it (cf. Matthew 27:18). If there had been any real basis for such charges, it would no doubt have come to Pilate's attention first. Furthermore, Pilate knew that the Sanhedrin would not be the ones to try Him for crimes such as those. After all, opposition to Roman taxation was well known and widespread among the Jewish leaders themselves. They once attempted to entrap Jesus on the issue of paying taxes to Caesar, and He had replied with the famous statement that had caused them to marvel at His wisdom: "Render to Caesar the things that are Caesar's, and to God the things that are God's" (Mark 12:17). So the charges against Him were lies. Jesus had never sought to establish a political kingdom in opposition to Rome, but quite the opposite (cf. John 6:15).

PILATE'S VERDICT

At this point, Pilate decided to bring Jesus into the Praetorium and examine Him. Matthew, Mark, and Luke all give a very abbreviated account of the examination: "Jesus stood before the governor. And the governor asked Him, saying, 'Are You the King of the Jews?' So Jesus said to him, 'It is as you say'" (Matthew 27:11).

John gives a fuller account of the exchange that took place:

Then Pilate entered the Praetorium again, called Jesus, and said to Him, "Are You the King of the Jews?" Jesus answered him, "Are you speaking for yourself about this, or did others tell you this concerning Me?" Pilate answered, "Am I a Jew? Your own nation and the chief priests have delivered You to me. What have You done?" Jesus answered, "My kingdom is not of this world. If My kingdom were of this world, My servants would fight, so that I should not be delivered to the Jews; but now My kingdom is not from here." Pilate therefore said to Him, "Are You a king then?" Jesus answered, "You say rightly that I am a king. For this cause I was born, and for this cause I have come into the world, that I should bear witness to the truth. Everyone who is of the truth hears My voice." (John 18:33–37)

Pilate clearly was aware that the Sanhedrin's charges against Jesus were baseless. But he was in a dilemma. On the one hand, he could not afford to aggravate the Sanhedrin. On the other hand, he did not want to be made their puppet. By bringing Jesus inside and questioning Him directly, he perhaps hoped to get a better assessment of the facts of the case, so that he could understand why the Sanhedrin felt Jesus posed such an urgent danger. Jesus' replies probably convinced Pilate that the whole matter was an internal religious dispute. It was clear that Jesus did claim to be a king. But it was also clear that His "kingdom" posed no immediate political threat to Rome.

The whole exchange seems to have only heightened Pilate's exasperation. He was evidently surprised and somewhat taken aback when Jesus answered his first question with a question. Pilate retorted with yet another question, then demanded that Jesus explain what He had done to merit so much animosity from the Sanhedrin. Jesus responded by answering Pilate's first question in a way that must have seemed cryptic to Pilate. He had no capacity for under-standing what Jesus meant by a kingdom that is "not of this world"—much less what He meant by "truth."

"Pilate said to Him, 'What is truth?'" (John 18:38). It was a rhe-torical question, merely an expression of Pilate's extreme frustration. It also reveals Pilate's cynical pragmatism about matters of truth. "Truth" to Pilate was defined in utilitarian terms. He stood ready to embrace as "truth" anything that advanced his political agenda. He was not interested in any other kind of truth—especially *spiritual* truth. He hadn't asked the question because he was looking for an answer. After all, the One who was Truth incarnate was standing before him, and if Pilate had been serious about seeking the truth, all he had to do was knock and the door would be opened to him (cf. Matthew 7:7–8). But what Pilate was really concerned about was finding a way out of the political dilemma the Sanhedrin had placed him in.

Pilate's real attitude toward "truth" is seen in the fact that he didn't even wait for a reply. "And when he had said this, he went out again to the Jews, and said to them, 'I find no fault in Him at all'" (John 18:38).

By then a crowd seems to have been forming at the Praetorium. The sight of the whole Sanhedrin marching Jesus through the streets, then standing outside Pilate's house while Pilate examined Him, could hardly have escaped the notice of Jerusalem's citizenry. Word was already getting around the city, and people were coming to find out what the fuss was all about. The Sanhedrin was perfectly posi-tioned to begin poisoning the well of public opinion by spreading rumors and accusations against Jesus as the crowd began to form. Because of the people's natural distrust of Roman authority, Pilate's unwillingness to do the Sanhedrin's bidding may have actually in-tensified the sentiment against Jesus. Furthermore, according to

Luke, when Pilate declared Jesus innocent, the members of the Sanhedrin "were the more fierce" in their accusations against Him (Luke 23:5).

JESUS' SILENCE

At this point, Jesus was probably being held by Roman soldiers next to Pilate on the balcony of the Praetorium. Matthew writes, "And while He was being accused by the chief priests and elders, He answered nothing. Then Pilate said to Him, 'Do You not hear how many things they testify against You?' But He answered him not one word, so that the governor marveled greatly" (Matthew 27:12–14).

Pilate knew full well that Jesus was innocent of the wrongs they accused Him of. He could see that the Sanhedrin was motivated by envy (v. 18). He had examined Jesus and found no fault in Him. He had already publicly pronounced Him innocent. The case should have been closed, Jesus should have been released, and Pilate should have dispersed the mob. But he was still too fearful of the political implications of offending the Sanhedrin.

Pilate had presided over countless criminal trials. He had seen hundreds—perhaps thousands—of accused criminals. *All* of them, innocent and guilty alike, vigorously protested their innocence at every opportunity. Never before had Pilate encountered anyone so manifestly innocent who nonetheless declined to speak in His own defense. Pilate was astonished and bewildered at Jesus' serene and majestic silence. He practically begged Jesus to lash back verbally at His accusers. But Jesus held His silence.

What was there to say? Whom was there to convince? What charges were on the table worth answering? Pilate had already declared Him innocent of any wrongdoing. The Sanhedrin also knew of His innocence and were simply determined to put Him to death anyway. It would have changed nothing for Jesus to speak in His own defense at this point, and so He held His peace.

Once again, this was all a perfect fulfillment of the divine plan. Hundreds of years before, Isaiah wrote of Christ's sacrificial self-offering: "He was oppressed and He was afflicted, yet He opened not His mouth; He was led as a lamb to the slaughter, and as a sheep before its shearers is silent, so He opened not His mouth" (Isaiah 53:7).

PILATE'S PREDICAMENT

Why didn't Pilate simply dismiss the case at once and send everyone home? Because the Sanhedrin had placed him in a very serious dilemma. He could not afford to offend them. Both his judgment and his fitness to rule Judea were already being questioned by his superiors in Rome. It was well known throughout the empire that the religious and political zeal of the Jews made Judea one of the most difficult of all Roman provinces to govern. The task required a statesman with the utmost maturity, tact, sound judgment, and an iron will. After four years of Pilate's rule in Judea, many in the Roman senate were not certain he was truly fit to be governor there.

Josephus records that Pilate got started off on the wrong foot soon after he was appointed to office, when he decided to contravene a longstanding Roman policy and have his armies carry their standards—featuring Caesar's likeness—into the city of Jerusalem. Previous governors had refrained from bringing any ensigns or emblems with Caesar's likeness into the city because of the Jews' deep conviction that all such images were idolatrous and in direct violation of the second commandment. Pilate, however, came to office with the conviction that it was time to enforce in Jerusalem the policies that were practiced everywhere else throughout the empire. On his orders, soldiers brought their standards into the city under cover of darkness one night soon after Pilate's governorship began. The next morning all Jerusalem awoke to the scandalous sight of Roman soldiers bearing Caesar's image.

The people of Jerusalem were incensed. A large horde of protestors traveled to Caesarea (where Pilate lived) to confront him directly about the policy. They implored him to remove the images from Jerusalem. Pilate, an angry and obdurate man, had no sympathy whatsoever for Jewish religious scruples and via a messenger declared his intention to leave the images in place. He refused even to meet with the protestors for five days. When the crowd persisted, Pilate, utterly exasperated, agreed to meet with them in the local amphitheater. It was merely a ploy to herd the protesters into a trap. Once there, Pilate ordered his soldiers to surround the crowd; then he threatened to behead them all if they did not cease and desist. It was a foolish and impetuous threat. There was no way Pilate could carry out such a massacre. But as far as the people of Israel were concerned, even if Pilate were serious about the threat, they were perfectly willing to die rather than allow Roman images to defile their holy city. Many of them deliberately bared their necks and fell to the ground before the sword-wielding soldiers.

Pilate was forced to yield, and the standards with Caesar's image were removed from Jerusalem. But neither the Roman senate nor Pilate's subjects were happy with his actions. He had been sent by Rome to Jerusalem to keep the peace, and yet one of his first acts had nearly provoked a riot. Moreover, his hot temper and lack of tact had almost turned the situation into a massacre. Pilate's superiors were not pleased. But the incident seemed to intensify Pilate's hatred of the Jewish religion, and throughout his reign, he deliberately did things that provoked the Jewish religious leaders.

On one occasion, for example, he used money from the temple treasury for the building of an aqueduct to Jerusalem. Some believed his real design was to supply water to an army in order to lay siege to the city. All of Jerusalem was once again in an uproar against him, and on Pilate's next visit to the city, a large crowd of protestors gathered. This time, knowing the folly of making threats he could not carry out, Pilate quelled the protest by sending soldiers into the crowd dressed as civilians. On Pilate's signal they drew clubs and swords from under their robes and forcibly dispersed the crowd, killing several people in the process.

Philo, a Hellenistic Jewish philosopher who was a contemporary of Jesus, recounted an incident in which Pilate had some gilded shields made and dedicated to Tiberius (who was Caesar at the time). He hung them in Herod's Jerusalem palace. (The palace probably had a wall where such honorific shields were supposed to be hung; it was a common way of honoring people at the time.) According to Philo, the shields contained only an inscription with the name of the person who donated the shield and the person who was being honored. However, Pilate had apparently used an inscription that referred to the emperor with all his traditional titles—one of which declared him "divine." The presence of the shields became highly offensive to the Jewish people. But this time the Jewish leaders threatened to appeal directly to Tiberius. According to Philo, they worded their threat in a most eloquent and subtle way:

> Do not cause a sedition; do not make war upon us; do not destroy the peace which exists. The honour of the emperor is not identical with dishonour to the ancient laws; let it not be to you a pretence for heaping insult on our nation. Tiberius is not desirous that any of our laws or customs shall be destroyed. And if you yourself say that he is, show us either some command from him, or some letter,

or something of the kind, that we, who have been sent to you as ambassadors, may cease to trouble you, and may address our supplications to your master.[1]

Pilate was both alarmed and outraged by the Jewish leaders' threat of an appeal to Tiberius, so he wrote to the emperor himself, setting forth an account of what had happened, obviously trying to paint himself in the most positive possible light. But Tiberius's response was what Pilate feared worst. He was furious with Pilate over the matter. In Philo's words:

Immediately, without putting any thing off till the next day, [Tiberius] wrote a letter reproaching and reviling [Pilate] in the most bitter manner for his act of unprecedented audacity and wickedness, and commanding him immediately to take down the shields and to convey them away from the metropolis of Judaea to Caesarea.[2]

In the course of recounting that incident, Philo gives a description of Pilate's character that certainly gives a fair measure of the reputation Pilate had among the Jews:

[Pilate] feared lest [the Jewish leaders] might in reality go on an embassy to the emperor, and might impeach him with respect to other particulars of his government, in respect of his corruption, and his acts of insolence, and his rapine, and his habit of insulting people, and his cruelty, and his continual murders of people untried and uncondemned, and his never ending and gratuitous, and most grievous inhumanity.[3]

Clearly, Pilate was a harsh and ruthless governor. Luke 13:1 mentions an incident involving some "Galileans whose blood Pilate had mingled with their sacrifices." That probably means he had them killed in the outer court of the temple while they were in Jerusalem to celebrate one of the feasts. They may have been particularly notorious insurrectionists, or they may have been agitators in some kind of riot. In any case, it provides one more example of why Pilate was so hated by those whom he ruled.

Yet it is clear that Pilate himself must have been deeply concerned by now about what Tiberius might do if his actions continued to provoke the Jewish people. One more notorious incident could result in Pilate's removal from office. As a matter of fact, that is precisely what eventually occurred. Just a few years after this, a certain false prophet duped a Samaritan religious sect into believing Moses had hidden the sacred vessels from the tabernacle on Mount Gerizim. The sect began gathering in a village near Gerizim, hoping to see the vessels. When Pilate heard about the gathering, he assumed the worst and ordered the Roman army to investigate what he presumed to be an insurrectionist movement. A slaughter ensued in which hundreds were slain who actually posed no threat to Rome whatsoever. The Samaritans appealed to the Roman legate in Syria (Pilate's immediate superior), and Pilate was called to Rome to answer the complaints against him. Before any hearing could occur, Tiberius died, and history records nothing more about Pilate—although legend suggests that he committed suicide.

HEROD'S TURN

It was obvious to everyone that Pilate was in a serious political predicament with Christ on trial before him. He had no legitimate grounds on which to execute Jesus, and yet he could not afford to anger the Jewish leaders over an issue they quite clearly regarded as urgent. For their part, the Sanhedrin were determined to press their charges against Jesus, knowing the leverage they had with Pilate, who didn't need any more bad press going back to Rome.

Suddenly an idea occurred to Pilate that might help him extricate himself from this dilemma. It was prompted by something someone said in one of the many accusations that were made against Jesus: "He stirs up the people, teaching throughout all Judea, beginning from Galilee to this place" (Luke 23:5). Galilee lay outside Pilate's area of jurisdiction. It belonged to the region ruled by Herod Antipas. Pilate realized that if Jesus were a Galilean, he might be able to hand the whole controversy off to Herod, who was also in town for Passover season. Luke writes,

> When Pilate heard of Galilee, he asked if the Man were a Galilean. And as soon as he knew that He belonged to Herod's jurisdiction, he sent Him to Herod, who was also in Jerusalem at that time. Now when Herod saw Jesus, he was exceedingly glad; for he had desired for a long time to see Him, because he had heard many things about Him, and he hoped to see some miracle done by Him. (vv. 6–8)

Herod's only interest in Jesus was idle curiosity. He had heard of the many miracles Jesus had done throughout Galilee, and he had long hoped to see Jesus do a miracle. Herod obviously thought of Jesus primarily as a potential source of amusement. Yet he was eager to see Him.

So Pilate had Jesus marched over to Herod's palace—a fairly short walk through the narrow city streets. By now more of the city would be awakening. The movement of the military escort, the Sanhedrin, and the accumulating crowd would have drawn still more people to see what was happening. Word began to spread through Jerusalem. Jesus was on trial. Throngs of curiosity seekers came to see for themselves.

No one was more curious or more eager to lay eyes on Jesus than Herod. Herod Antipas was the same member of the Herodian dynasty who had killed John the Baptist a couple of years before (Matthew 14:1–12). His main palace was located in the city of Tiberias, a spectacular, sparkling, new town on the west shore of the Sea of Galilee, only ten miles or so from Capernaum (Peter's hometown and Jesus' base of operations). Herod himself had built Tiberias less than ten years before. He had named it in honor of Caesar. Josephus records that when the foundations for the city were being dug, an ancient graveyard was uncovered. Therefore in Jesus' day the city was deemed defiled, and no law-abiding Jewish person would set foot there. The city was mainly inhabited by Romans and other foreigners.

Jesus' ministry covered the entire Galilee region, but there is no mention in Scripture that He ever visited Tiberias. It may be that Jesus was deliberately keeping His distance from Herod. Herod's palace in Tiberias was most likely the very place where John the Baptist was beheaded. There were rumors that Herod was also seeking to kill Jesus. And while it is clear that Jesus was not intimidated by Herod, He knew He had to die in Jerusalem, so that the Scriptures might be fulfilled (Luke 13:31–33). Therefore, even though Herod and Jesus had lived quite literally within walking distance of each other for several years, and Herod was well familiar with Jesus' reputation, this was Herod's first opportunity to see Jesus with his own eyes.

How different Christ must have looked from the strong, prophetic miracle worker Herod expected to see! His face was already badly bruised and swollen from the abuse He had taken. Spittle and blood were drying in His matted hair. Tired and physically weakened from a sleepless night, He stood before Herod, bound and under guard like a common criminal.

Most disappointing to Herod was Jesus' refusal to perform for him. Herod "questioned Him with many words, but He answered him nothing" (Luke 23:9). The Sanhedrin was still dogging Christ, standing nearby and vehemently shouting denunciation and accusations at Him (v. 10). But Jesus refused to utter even so much as a word. In *all* the various hearings and examinations He was subjected to, He was astonishingly quiet (cf. Matthew 27:14)—always refusing to rail at His accusers or say anything in self-defense (1 Peter 2:23). But only before Herod did He remain in utter and complete silence. In the first place, Herod had no legitimate jurisdiction in Jerusalem. If Herod intended to impose any sentence in this case, Jesus would first have to be taken back to Galilee and put on trial there. So Jesus had no legal obligation to answer him anyway. But there may have been another reason Jesus kept silent. Herod's treatment of Jesus' forerunner, John the Baptist, made clear where he stood regarding the truth of Christ. For Jesus to answer him would have been like giving what is holy to the dogs, or casting pearls before swine. Herod was already poised to turn and tear Christ in pieces (cf. Matthew 7:6). Silence was the only appropriate response under such circumstances.

After a short time, Herod grew tired of questioning Jesus and decided to make sport of Him. "Then Herod, with his men of war, treated Him with contempt and mocked Him, arrayed Him in a gorgeous robe, and sent Him back to Pilate" (Luke 23:11). Luke adds a historical footnote: "That very day Pilate and Herod became friends with each other, for previously they had been at enmity with each other" (v. 12). It was an unholy alliance—a friendship based on the one thing they had in common: their cowardly and contemptuous treatment of Christ.

Both Herod and Pilate knew that Christ posed no immediate threat to their political interests. His appearance and his demeanor spoke for themselves. How could such a passive, serene, fragile person— whose claim to fame was as a teacher and a healer—pose any political threat to anyone? It was as clear to Herod as it had been to Pilate that the Sanhedrin's charges were fabricated and ill-motivated. But Herod happily joined in the game. He clothed Jesus in a gorgeous robe (probably one of Herod's own hand-me-downs, or a gift that Herod did not care about). Then Herod and his security forces subjected Him to mockery and contempt before the growing crowd of onlookers.

Finally, after satisfying his desire for amusement at the expense of Jesus, Herod sent Him back to Pilate.

THE CROWD'S HOSTILITY

Jesus' own refusal to speak to Herod helped force the trial back into Pilate's court. Pilate must have been surprised and somewhat frustrated when the Sanhedrin returned with Jesus and a larger-than-ever crowd of onlookers in tow. Things were only getting further out of hand, and now it would be harder than ever for Pilate to end the matter without creating a scandal that might get back to Rome—or worse, starting a riot on the busiest day of the year in Jerusalem. Either way, Pilate's career could be jeopardized by this.

Pilate therefore decided to try to act the statesman and bring an end to the matter with a compromise of sorts. Luke says,

> Then Pilate, when he had called together the chief priests, the rulers, and the people, said to them, "You have brought this Man to me, as one who misleads the people. And indeed, having examined Him in your presence, I have found no fault in this Man concerning those things of which you accuse Him; no, neither did Herod, for I sent you back to him; and indeed nothing deserving of death has been done by Him. I will therefore chastise Him and release Him." (Luke 23:13–16)

In other words, Pilate proposed to punish Jesus with a Roman scourge—even though he found Him guilty of nothing—as a compromise gesture. After that, he hoped to release Jesus.

Pilate actually proposed Jesus' release in fulfillment of a custom that was in place at the time. As a diplomatic gesture toward the Jews, and in order to promote goodwill on the feast day, the Roman governor would release one Jewish prisoner from Roman custody every Passover. This was most likely a longstanding tradition that dated back even before Pilate's administration. Matthew says, "Now at the feast the governor was accustomed to releasing to the multitude one prisoner whom they wished" (Matthew 27:15). Matthew is not suggesting that the Roman governor would automatically release *whomever* the people wished, allowing them to choose from all the prisoners in custody at the time. Instead, what he means is that a few offenders were selected by Roman officials and those names were given to the people as candidates from which to choose. Rome would grant an automatic pardon to the prisoner the people selected from the names proposed to them.

Pilate seems to have decided to use the custom for his own benefit in a last-ditch effort to escape the dilemma the Sanhedrin had created for him—a conflict between conscience and career; a choice between satisfying the Jews he hated or the Caesar he feared. He gave the people a choice of only *two* prisoners to be released. One was Jesus, whose popularity among the common people was well known. After all, less than a week before this, all Jerusalem (it seemed) turned out to welcome Him to the city and shout hosannas as He entered in a procession the people fashioned for Him. Pilate could hardly have been unaware of Jesus' popularity.

The only other candidate for release Pilate gave them was Barabbas, a miscreant so foul and notorious that Pilate seemed sure the people would never choose him. Matthew's narrative continues: "And at that time they had a notorious prisoner called Barabbas. Therefore, when they had gathered together, Pilate said to them, 'Whom do you want me to release to you? Barabbas, or Jesus who is called Christ?'" (Matthew 27:16–17).

Barabbas had been convicted of murder, sedition, and robbery (Luke 23:25; John 18:40). His crimes had made him infamous, and he was probably both hated and feared by the people. Pilate probably thought his clever ploy would leave the people with no option but to choose Jesus' release over that of Barabbas. That way Pilate could avoid complicity in the Sanhedrin's plot against Jesus. ("For he knew that they had handed Him over because of envy"—Matthew 27:18.) This way, Pilate could release Jesus, but rather than being seen as refusing to carry out the will of the Sanhedrin, he would be seen as obeying the will of the people. It was a brilliant diplomatic maneuver.

But it did not work.

First of all, just as Pilate was preparing to render his final verdict, the scene was interrupted in a most unusual way. "While he was sitting on the judgment seat, his wife sent to him, saying, 'Have nothing to do with that just Man, for I have suffered many things today in a dream because of Him'" (v. 19). Apparently the message was delivered publicly, so that all present could hear. Thus it served as a warning not only to Pilate but also to the Sanhedrin and the people. God in His merciful providence orchestrated both the dream and the timing of Mrs. Pilate's warning so that all concerned would have one final, gracious alarm-beacon before they proceeded with the monstrously evil deed they planned to carry out.

As far as Pilate was concerned, his wife's warning only heightened his dilemma. The pressure on him from both sides was increasing, and he was more eager than ever to lay the whole issue to rest.

But the moment court was interrupted by Pilate's wife's message, the Sanhedrin seized the opportunity to rally the people around their cause. They began to spread the word to the crowd that they should choose Barabbas. "The chief priests and elders persuaded the multitudes that they should ask for Barabbas and destroy Jesus" (v. 20). The Sanhedrin was comprised of the spiritual leaders of the land. For them to manipulate the people like this was a gross abuse of their God-given authority. But they found the crowd perfectly willing to be led astray.

Pilate posed the question one more time: "The governor answered and said to them, 'Which of the two do you want me to release to you?' They said, 'Barabbas!'" (v. 21). The answer came back clearly and unanimously, without hesitation.

Pilate was dumbfounded. He asked them, "'What then shall I do with Jesus who is called Christ?' They all said to him, 'Let Him be crucified!'" (v. 22).

Pilate, still unable to believe that the entire mob would have such strong feelings against One who had so lately been so popular, asked, "'Why, what evil has He done?' But they cried out all the more, saying, 'Let Him be crucified!'" (v. 23).

THE GOVERNOR'S ACQUIESCENCE

It was clear that the bloodthirsty crowd would be satisfied with nothing less than the destruction of Jesus. It mattered nothing to them that no legitimate charges had been brought against Him. They cared little about truth or justice. They wanted a crucifixion. Many in the crowd were blindly following the lead of the Sanhedrin, but there were undoubtedly many others who hated Jesus for all the same reasons people today hate Him: His teaching confronted their wicked lifestyles; His demands were too hard; the truth He taught was too narrow for their tastes. The real issue, in every case, was that "Men loved darkness rather than light, because their deeds were evil" (John 3:19).

Pilate had reached the end of his rope. He had no desire to participate in the conspiracy against Jesus, but the Jewish leaders had left him little choice. The crowd was now on the verge of a riot. He was finally out of options. Matthew writes, "When Pilate saw that he could not prevail at all, but rather that a tumult was rising, he took water and washed his hands before the multitude, saying, 'I am innocent of the blood of this just Person. You see to it'" (Matthew 27:24).

The ceremonial hand washing was a Jewish ritual, and its meaning would have been poignantly familiar to the crowd. Pilate was expressing contempt for the fact that they had railroaded him into becoming a part of the conspiracy against Jesus. He was giving them what they wanted, but he wanted to make it clear that he was not doing it willingly.

Of course, no ritual hand washing could truly absolve Pilate of the guilt he bore for his part in the crucifixion. He had the power and the responsibility to stop it, but he did not. He was as guilty as the rest, and the fact that he participated out of political expediency rather than overt hatred for Jesus did not nullify or minimize his guilt in the least.

For their part, the people would have been perfectly happy to absolve Pilate. "All the people answered and said, 'His blood be on us and on our children'" (v. 25). In an amazing act of self-condemnation, they said they would accept the full blame on themselves and their posterity, if that was what it took to get Pilate to let them kill Jesus.

Of course, their *saying* that Pilate was absolved from the guilt did not make it so. Scripture makes it perfectly clear that Pilate, Herod, the people of Jerusalem, and the Gentiles who participated in the crucifixion all bore the guilt together (Acts 4:27). But it is an interesting fact of history that just a few short months after this, the same Jewish leaders who had provoked the people to say, "His blood be on us and on our children," were resentful of the disciples' gospel preaching, saying, "You have filled Jerusalem with your doctrine, and intend to bring this Man's blood on us!" (Acts 5:28).

Pilate had originally hoped to have Jesus flogged and released. According to John's Gospel, Pilate was still seeking a way to release Him, and that may be why he had Him publicly scourged at this point. Perhaps he thought the sight of a Roman scourging would satisfy the crowd's bloodlust.

Scourging alone was sometimes fatal. A Roman scourge was a short wooden handle with numerous long lashes of leather attached to it. Each leather strip had a sharp piece of glass, metal, bone, or other hard object attached to the end of it. The victim would be stripped of all clothing and tied to a post by his wrists with his hands high enough over his head to virtually lift him off the ground. The feet would be dangling, and the skin on the back and buttocks completely taut. One or two scourge-bearers (lictors) would then deliver blows, skillfully laying the lashes diagonally across the back and buttocks with extreme force. The skin would literally be torn away, and often muscles were deeply lacerated. It was not uncommon for the scourge-wounds to penetrate deep into the kidneys or lacerate arteries, causing wounds that in themselves proved fatal. Some victims died from extreme shock during the flogging.

The apostle John records how after Jesus' scourging and the mockery that accompanied it, Pilate once more vainly tried to seek Jesus' release. Pilate brought Jesus again before the crowd, dressed in a robe fashioned from a soldier's tunic, crowned with a crown of thorns, and triumphantly presented Him to the people, probably hoping they would be satisfied that Jesus had suffered enough: "And Pilate said to them, 'Behold the Man!'" (John 19:5).

But they were not satisfied. "Therefore, when the chief priests and officers saw Him, they cried out, saying, 'Crucify Him, crucify Him!'" (v. 6).

Pilate, still astonished at the crowd's insatiable thirst for Jesus' blood, said to them, "You take Him and crucify Him, for I find no fault in Him" (v. 6). Still vainly trying to wash his hands of the matter, he repeated his earlier verdict, declaring Jesus' innocence once more.

But the crowd would have none of it. "The Jews answered him, 'We have a law, and according to our law He ought to die, because He made Himself the Son of God.' Therefore, when Pilate heard that saying, he was the more afraid, and went again into the Praetorium, and said to Jesus, 'Where are You from?'" (vv. 7–9). They were demanding that Pilate follow through with a crucifixion at the hands of Roman authorities. Their mention of His claim to be the Son of God seems to have severely rattled Pilate. His question to Jesus ("Where are you from?") was obviously spoken with a mixture of wonder, amazement, and fear.

"But Jesus gave him no answer" (v. 9).

"Then Pilate said to Him, 'Are You not speaking to me? Do You not know that I have power to crucify You, and power to release You?' Jesus answered, 'You could have no power at all against Me unless it had been given you from above. Therefore the one who delivered Me to you has the greater sin'" (vv. 10–11).

Pilate was by now beginning to see the enormity of his wrongdoing from Jesus' perspective. Perhaps it was merely a superstitious fear on Pilate's part, but he was clearly shaken by Jesus' claim of deity (for Pilate would have correctly understood the implications of the expression "Son of God"). And he wanted no part of the guilt he knew he would bear if such a claim were true, because he had already wrongfully abused Jesus merely by having Him flogged. And even though Pilate was not a believer in the Hebrew God, his Roman polytheistic world-view was laden with superstition about offending the gods and the heavy price one could pay for such an offense.

Furthermore, it must have sent a cold shiver down Pilate's spine when Jesus told him, with quiet composure and a calm, unflappable authority, "You could have no power at all against Me unless it had been given you from above." That seems to be why "From then on Pilate sought to release Him" (v. 12).

"But the Jews cried out, saying, 'If you let this Man go, you are not Caesar's friend. Whoever makes himself a king speaks against Caesar'" (v. 12). This was their trump card against Pilate, and it was a plain statement of the consistent line of argument they had been pressing on him from the beginning. This is why they had so much leverage against him: they knew he was concerned about what Caesar would think, and he was especially afraid of what all this could ultimately mean for his career. But the crowd's threat against Pilate was full of irony, since not one of *them* wanted to be thought of as "Caesar's friend." Still, it was an effective, though not very subtle, threat.

"When Pilate therefore heard that saying, he brought Jesus out and sat down in the judgment seat in a place that is called The Pavement, but in Hebrew, Gabbatha" (John 19:13). The Pavement was a stone-paved area adjacent to the Antonio Fortress, where military court was sometimes held and prisoners were detained. The paving stones are there to this day, and some of them still bear marks where Roman soldiers played games like tic-tac-toe while guarding prisoners during hearings. Since the Jewish leaders would not enter Pilate's judgment hall in the Praetorium, Pilate had Jesus taken to Gabbatha for His final judgment. There was a judgment seat there where Pilate could render his final official orders.

John writes,

Now it was the Preparation Day of the Passover, and about the sixth hour. And he said to the Jews, "Behold your King!" But they cried out, "Away with Him, away with Him! Crucify Him!" Pilate said to them, "Shall I crucify your King?" The chief priests answered, "We have no king but Caesar!" Then he delivered Him to them to be crucified. So they took Jesus and led Him away. (John 19:14–16)

The sixth hour, by Roman calculation, would be 6:00 A.M., so it was still an extremely early hour. The crowd persisted in their cries for Jesus' crucifixion. Pilate had finally been forced into precisely the circumstances he so desperately wanted to avoid. But he now felt he had no choice, and so he gave the order for Jesus to be crucified. He bartered away his eternal soul for temporary job security.

Rome was thus in full complicity with the Sanhedrin's murderous scheme. Pilate, the highest ruler in the region, had been utterly unable to derail the crucifixion. There was no stopping it now.

ENDNOTES
  1 Philo, *Legatio ad Gaium*, 301.
  2 Philo, *Legatio ad Gaium*, 305.
  3 Philo, *Legatio ad Gaium*, 302.

10

And He, bearing His cross, went out to a place called the Place of a Skull, which is called in Hebrew, Golgotha, where they crucified Him, and two others with Him, one on either side, and Jesus in the center.

—JOHN 19:17–18

10

⚜ Murder at Golgotha

THE FLOGGING administered by Pilate was merely the beginning of a long series of physical and emotional tortures that would finally culminate in the death of Jesus. It was accompanied by cruel mockery, which the pagan Roman soldiers apparently administered purely for their own amusement. Matthew describes the scene:

> Then he released Barabbas to them; and when he had scourged Jesus, he delivered Him to be crucified. Then the soldiers of the governor took Jesus into the Praetorium and gathered the whole garrison around Him. And they stripped Him and put a scarlet robe on Him. When they had twisted a crown of thorns, they put it on His head, and a reed in His right hand. And they bowed the knee before Him and mocked Him, saying, "Hail, King of the Jews!" Then they spat on Him, and took the reed and struck Him on the head. (Matthew 27:26–30)

Despite the fact that these soldiers had no reason whatsoever to heap such scorn on Jesus, they evidently took great delight in doing so. These were men hardened by having witnessed numerous executions, so the pain of such torture no longer made any impact whatsoever on them. As far as they were concerned, Jesus was merely another religious fanatic with whom they were free to amuse themselves as cruelly as they pleased.

It seemed as if the whole world was against Jesus. Jews and Gentiles alike were now willfully, even gleefully, participating in His murder, determined to see Him die in the most agonizing way possible. A catalogue of the pains of crucifixion would fill an entire volume, but Scripture lays particular stress on several aspects of the tortures Christ endured.

THE MOCKERY

The Roman soldiers had no idea whom they were tormenting. As far as they were concerned, they were simply crucifying another criminal under orders from Pilate, their commander-in-chief.

Pilate's orders were to scourge and crucify Jesus, but the cruel mockery they heaped on Him reveals their own wickedness. As they led Jesus back to the Praetorium, they deliberately made a spectacle of Him for the amusement of the taunting crowd. The tumult drew the entire garrison of soldiers to watch.

A Roman cohort consisted of six hundred soldiers. These soldiers were stationed at the Antonio Fortress (which overlooked the temple mount from the north). They were an elite unit, assigned to serve the governor and to keep the peace that was so fragile in this most volatile region of the Roman empire. Rome conscripted soldiers from all the regions she conquered, but Jews were exempt from military service, so all these soldiers would have been Gentiles. They were probably Syrian troops, because Syrians spoke Aramaic, and this would have been essential in Jerusalem. Some of these same soldiers were undoubtedly part of the group who had arrested Jesus in Gethsemane the previous night. Still, they probably had little knowledge of who He was. As far as they were concerned, He was just one in a long line of religious zealots who had troubled the peace and made problems for Rome. They undoubtedly assumed that He deserved whatever ridicule and torment they could heap on Him. Condemned Roman prisoners were considered fair game for such abuse, as long as they were not killed before the sentence of crucifixion could be carried out. The soldiers' abuse of Jesus was probably not motivated by any personal animosity toward Him, but it was nonetheless wicked in the extreme. The soldiers had become experts at such mockery, having overseen so many executions—but rarely did they have such enthusiastic crowds to play to. They evidently decided to make the most of it.

Jesus had already been slapped and beaten repeatedly, even before He was delivered to Pilate, so his face was undoubtedly swollen and bleeding already. After the scourging, His back would be a mass of bleeding wounds and quivering muscles, and the robe they fashioned for Him would only add to the pain of those wounds. They stripped Him of His own garments, which suggests He was quite literally naked apart from the robe they fashioned for Him. The robe was apparently made from an old tunic—probably an old garment that had been discarded by one of the soldiers. (The Greek expression is *chlamus,* signifying a military cloak; not the same "gorgeous robe"—*esthes*—used by Herod in Luke 23:11). Matthew says the robe was scarlet, but Mark and John call it "purple," (Mark 15:17; John 19:2)—suggesting that it was a badly faded tunic. It was probably the nearest thing to purple (signifying royalty) the soldiers could find.

Their aim was clearly to make a complete mockery of His claim that He was a king. To that end, they fashioned a crown of thorns.

Caesar wore a laurel wreath as a crown; thorns were a cruel corruption of that. These were no doubt the longest, sharpest thorns that could be found; many varieties of these grow in Jerusalem to this day—some with two-inch barbed quills that would penetrate deep into His head as the crown was pressed hard upon Him.

The reed in His hand was a further attempt to lampoon His royal claim. The reed represented a scepter—but was a weak, frail imitation of the scepter Caesar carried on festive state occasions.

Jesus' silence may have convinced them that He was merely a madman, and they showed their utter contempt for Him by feigning the sort of veneration one would show to royalty, bowing at His feet, but saying "Hail, King of the Jews!" in jeering tones. Then, as the Jewish priests had done, they spat on Him, and one of them took the reed from his hand and used it to strike Him repeatedly on His head. The reed, though a flimsy scepter, would have been firm enough to inflict great pain on His already battered head. The apostle John records that they also struck Him with their hands (John 19:3)—probably slapping with open hands while taunting Him some more.

They were clearly playing to the crowd of onlookers. And the crowd was probably cheering them on. But the soldiers were utterly ignorant about who He really was. He is indeed King of kings, and one day He will quite literally rule the world. But His rightful scepter is no reed; it is a rod of iron (Psalm 2:9; Revelation 19:15). One day, according to Scripture, it will be God who mocks the wicked.

> *He who sits in the heavens shall laugh;*
> *The LORD shall hold them in derision.*
> *Then He shall speak to them in His wrath,*
> *And distress them in His deep displeasure:*
> *"Yet I have set My King on My holy hill of Zion."*

> PSALM 2:4–6

If they had truly known who He was, there is no way they would have treated Him in such a fashion.

But Jesus held His silence. "When He was reviled, [He] did not revile in return; when He suffered, He did not threaten, but committed Himself to Him who judges righteously" (1 Peter 2:23). Jesus knew these things were part of God's own plan for Him, so He suffered them all willingly, patiently, and unperturbedly.

THE SHAME

"And when they had mocked Him, they took the robe off Him, put His own clothes on Him, and led Him away to be crucified" (Matthew 27:31). Victims of crucifixion were usually made to wear a placard around the neck on which was written the crime they were condemned for. It was part of the shame that was deliberately inflicted on victims of crucifixion (cf. Hebrews 12:2; 13:13). They were led through the streets and made to walk in a public procession in order to maximize the humiliation of the spectacle.

They were also forced to carry their own cross to the place of execution. That practice was what Jesus referred to earlier in his ministry when He told the disciples, "Whoever desires to come after Me, let him deny himself, and take up his cross, and follow Me" (Mark 8:34). Some have suggested that Roman victims were made to carry only the lateral crossbeam (known as the *patibulum),* which was later attached to the top of a vertical beam, which was already planted firmly in the ground. But Scripture seems to indicate that Christ was bearing the entire cross. A Roman cross large enough to crucify a grown man might weigh as much as two hundred pounds—an extremely heavy load to bear in any circumstances. But for someone in Jesus' already weakened condition it would be virtually impossible to drag such a load from the Praetorium to a place of crucifixion outside the walls of Jerusalem.

As a matter of fact, Matthew records that Jesus needed help bearing His cross: "Now as they came out, they found a man of Cyrene, Simon by name. Him they compelled to bear His cross" (27:32). At least four soldiers—a quaternion—would accompany the victim to the execution site. The soldiers evidently grew impatient with Jesus' agonizing pace, and they grabbed Simon along the way, conscripting him to carry the cross for Jesus.

Jesus' exhaustion is completely understandable. Remember that the previous day had been so grueling that His disciples had been unable to stay awake while Jesus prayed in the garden. But that was only the *beginning* of extreme agony for Jesus. He literally sweated blood in His intense grief and sorrow while He prayed. Then He was arrested, beaten repeatedly, held without sleep all night, beaten some more, flogged by a Roman scourge, beaten and mocked again. After several hours of such sheer agony, combined with blood loss and shock, it is no wonder He was too weak to carry a two-hundred-pound cross to Calvary by Himself.

Even with Simon carrying His cross, Jesus apparently was too weak to walk unsupported. Mark 15:22 says, "they brought Him to the place Golgotha," using a Greek expression for "brought" that suggests He was actually borne along to that place—probably walking with much difficulty, needing constant support from the soldiers along the way.

Simon the Cyrene was no idle spectator wishing to mock Jesus like the rest of the crowd. Mark 15:21 says, "He was coming out of the country and passing by." As Jesus was leaving the city, Simon was apparently entering, and by divine appointment, he was at exactly the right place at the right moment to be of help to Jesus.

Cyrene was an African city on the Mediterranean coast—in what is Libya today. A large Jewish community lived there, and Simon was probably a Jewish pilgrim who had made the long journey from Cyrene to Jerusalem for the Passover. Mark identifies Simon as "the father of Alexander and Rufus" (v. 21). Mark was probably writing from Rome around A.D. 50, so Alexander and Rufus were probably believers known to the church there. (Paul sent greetings to "Rufus, chosen in the Lord, and his mother" in Romans 16:13. If it is the same Rufus, his mother would have been Simon's wife). The fact that Simon is named in all three synoptic gospels suggests that his later history was known to the gospel writers, and that undoubtedly means he later became a believer in Christ. Though he could not have been pleased about being conscripted to carry a condemned criminal's cross, it became a doorway to eternal life for him.

Christ's last public message was given on the road to Calvary. Luke describes it:

> And a great multitude of the people followed Him, and women who also mourned and lamented Him. But Jesus, turning to them, said, "Daughters of Jerusalem, do not weep for Me, but weep for yourselves and for your children. For indeed the days are coming in which they will say, 'Blessed are the barren, wombs that never bore, and breasts which never nursed!' Then they will begin 'to say to the mountains, "Fall on us!" and to the hills, "Cover us!"' For if they do these things in the green wood, what will be done in the dry?" (23:27–31)

Part of the message was a reference to Hosea 10:8 ("They shall say to the mountains, 'Cover us!' And to the hills, 'Fall on us!'"). It was a dire warning of disaster to come. Since in that culture childbearing was understood to be the highest blessing God could give a woman, only the worst kind of plague or disaster could ever cause anyone to say "Blessed are the barren, wombs that never bore, and breasts which never nursed!"

The green tree represented a time of abundance and blessing, and the dry tree stood for bad times. Jesus was saying that if a tragedy like this could happen in good times, what would befall the nation in bad times? If the Romans crucified someone whom they admitted was guilty of no offense, what would they do to the Jewish nation when they rebelled? Christ was referring to events that would happen less than a generation later, in A.D. 70, when the Roman army would lay siege to Jerusalem, utterly destroy the temple, and slaughter thousands upon thousands of Jewish people—multitudes of them by crucifixion. Christ had spoken of the coming holocaust before (cf. Luke 19:41–44). His awareness of that approaching catastrophe—and the knowledge that some of these same people and their children would suffer in it—still weighed heavily on His mind as He made His way to the cross.

THE CURSE

In the Jewish mind crucifixion was a particularly execrable way to die. It was tantamount to the hanging on a tree Moses described in Deuteronomy 21:22–23: "If a man has committed a sin deserving of death, and he is put to death, and you hang him on a tree, his body shall not remain overnight on the tree, but you shall surely bury him that day, so that you do not defile the land which the LORD your God is giving you as an inheritance; for he who is hanged is accursed of God." The Mosaic law also required that all executions occur outside the city walls (Numbers 15:35; cf. Hebrews 13:12).

The Romans had a slightly different concept. They made sure that all crucifixions took place near major thoroughfares in order to make the condemned person a public example for all passersby. So Jesus' crucifixion took place outside the city, but in a heavily trafficked location carefully selected to make Him a public spectacle.

The place where Jesus was crucified was called Calvary (a Latin adaptation of the Greek term that appears in the biblical text: *kranion,* "a skull"—Luke 23:33). The Aramaic name for it was Golgotha, also meaning, "a skull." Nowhere in Scripture is it called a hill, but it is generally assumed that this spoke of a promontory, craggy knoll, or incline that had the appearance of a skull. There is such a place, known as Gordon's Calvary, just north of Jerusalem's city walls. It still can be seen today and still bears an uncanny resemblance to a human skull.

Matthew writes, "And when they had come to a place called Golgotha, that is to say, Place of a Skull, they gave Him sour wine mingled with gall to drink. But when He had tasted it, He would not drink" (Matthew 27:33–34). Apparently just before they nailed Him to the cross, the soldiers offered Him this bitter drink. "Sour wine" is vinegar. "Gall" is something that tastes bitter. Mark 15:23 says the bitter substance was myrrh, which acts as a mild narcotic. The soldiers may have offered it for its numbing effect just before they drove the nails through the flesh. When Jesus tasted what it was, He spat it out. He did not want His senses numbed. He had come to the cross to be a sin bearer, and He would feel the full effect of the sin He bore; He would endure the full measure of its pain. The Father had given Him a cup to drink more bitter than the gall of myrrh, but without the stupefying effect. His heart was still steadfastly set on doing the will of the Father, and He would not anesthetize His senses before He had accomplished all His work.

The vinegar and gall fulfilled a Messianic prophecy from Psalm 69:19–21:

> *You know my reproach, my shame, and my dishonor;*
> *My adversaries are all before You.*
> *Reproach has broken my heart,*

And I am full of heaviness;
I looked for someone to take pity, but there was none;
And for comforters, but I found none.
They also gave me gall for my food,
And for my thirst they gave me vinegar to drink.

THE PAIN

"Then they crucified Him" (Matthew 27:35). Crucifixion was a form of execution that the Romans had learned from the Persians. It was also practiced in pre-Roman times in Phoenicia, Carthage, and Egypt. But it evidently originated in Persia. The Persians' believed that earth, fire, and water were sacred elements, and all customary methods of execution defiled the sacred elements. So the Persians developed a method of crucifying victims by impaling them on a pole, thus raising them high above the earth, where they were left to die. Later cultures developed different methods of crucifixion, and Rome employed several of them. By the time of Christ, crucifixion had become the favorite method of execution throughout the Roman empire, and especially in Judea, where it was regularly used to make a public example of rioters and insurrectionists. According to Josephus, after Herod the Great died, the Roman governor of Syria, Quinctilius Varus, crucified two thousand men in order to quell an uprising. Josephus also says that Titus crucified so many people when he sacked Jerusalem in A.D. 70 that there was no wood left for crosses and no place left to set them up. By the time of Christ alone, Rome had already crucified more than thirty thousand victims in and around Judea. So crosses with dead or dying men hanging on them were a common sight around Jerusalem, and a constant reminder of Roman brutality.

The exact process used in Jesus' crucifixion is a matter of some conjecture. None of the gospel accounts gives a detailed description of the method used on Him. But we can glean quite a lot of information from the incidental details that are given. From Thomas's remark to the other disciples after the crucifixion ("Unless I see in His hands the print of the nails, and put my finger into the print of the nails . . . I will not believe"—John 20:25) we learn that Christ was nailed to the cross, rather than being lashed by leather thongs, as was sometimes done. From Matthew 27:37, which states that His indictment was posted "over His head," we deduce that the form of cross He was nailed to was the familiar *crux imissa,* where the top of the upright protruded above the *patibulum,* rather than the often-used St. Anthony's Cross, a T-shaped stake.

We also can glean from secular accounts of crucifixion in Jesus' time some of the details about how crucifixion victims died. Christ would have been nailed to the cross as it lay flat on the ground. The nails used were long, tapered iron spikes, similar to modern railroad spikes, but much sharper. The nails had to be driven through the wrists (not the palms of the hands), because neither the tendons nor the bone structure in the hands could support the body's weight. Nails in the palms would simply tear the flesh between the bones. Nails through the wrists would usually shatter carpal bones and tear the carpal ligaments, but the structure of the wrist was nonetheless strong enough to support the weight of the body. As the nail went into the wrist, it would usually cause severe damage to the sensorimotor median nerve, causing intense pain in both arms. Finally, a single nail would be driven through both feet, sometimes through the Achilles' tendons. None of the nail wounds would be fatal, but they would all cause intense and increasing pain as the victim's time on the cross dragged on.

After the victim was nailed in place, several soldiers would slowly elevate the top of the cross and carefully slide the foot into a deep posthole. The cross would drop with a jarring blow into the bottom of the hole, causing the full weight of the victim to be immediately borne by the nails in the wrists and feet. That would cause a bone-wrenching pain throughout the body, as major joints were suddenly twisted out of their natural position. That is probably what Christ referred to prophetically in Psalm 22, a psalm about the crucifixion: "I am poured out like water, and all My bones are out of joint" (v. 14).

The Romans had perfected the art of crucifixion in order to maximize the pain—and they knew how to prolong the horror without permitting the victim to lapse into a state of unconsciousness that might relieve the pain. The victim of crucifixion would experience waves of nausea, fever, intense thirst, constant cramps, and incessant, throbbing pain from all parts of the body. Sleeplessness, hunger, dehydration, and worsening infection all took their toll on the victim's body and spirit as the process of crucifixion dragged on—usually for three days or so. The feeling of utter hopelessness, the public shame, and the ever-increasing trauma to the body all intensified as the hours dragged on. One author wrote,

The unnatural position made every movement painful; the lacerated veins and crushed tendons throbbed with incessant anguish; the wounds, inflamed by exposure, gradually gangrened; the arteries—especially at the head and stomach—became swollen and oppressed with surcharged blood; and while each variety of misery went on gradually increasing, there was added to them the intolerable pang of burning and raging thirst; and all these physical complications caused an internal excitement and anxiety, which made the prospect of death itself—of death, the awful unknown enemy, at whose approach man usually shudders most—bear the aspect of a delicious and exquisite release.[1]

The emperor Tiberius is said to have preferred crucifixion as a method of punishment, precisely because it prolonged the victim's agony without granting relief by death. He believed death was an escape, so in his view execution was really no *punishment*, unless the victim had as much mortal agony inflicted as possible *before* death.

Death normally came from slow suffocation. The victim's body would hang in such a way that the diaphragm was severely constricted. In order to exhale, he would have to push up with the feet so that the diaphragm would have room to move. Ultimately fatigue, intense pain, or muscle atrophy would render the victim unable to do this, and he would finally die from the lack of oxygen. Truman Davis, a medical doctor who studied the physical effects of crucifixion, described how this would have occurred in Jesus' crucifixion:

> As the arms fatigue, great waves of cramps sweep over the muscles, knotting them in deep, relentless, throbbing pain. With these cramps comes the inability to push Himself upward. Hanging by His arms, the pectoral muscles are paralyzed and the intercostal muscles are unable to act. Air can be drawn into the lungs, but cannot be exhaled. Jesus fights to raise Himself in order to get even one short breath. Finally, carbon dioxide builds up in the lungs and in the blood stream and the cramps partially subside. Spasmodically He is able to push Himself upward to exhale and bring in the life-giving oxygen. . . .
>
> Hours of this limitless pain, cycles of twisting, joint-rending cramps, intermittent partial asphyxiation, searing pain as tissue is torn from His lacerated back as He moves up and down against the rough timber; then another agony begins. A deep crushing pain in the chest as the pericardium slowly fills with serum and begins to compress the heart.
>
> It is now almost over—the loss of tissue fluid has reached a critical level—the compressed heart is struggling to pump heavy, thick,

sluggish blood into the tissues—the tortured lungs are making a frantic effort to gasp in small gulps of air. The markedly dehydrated tissues send their flood of stimuli to the brain.[2]

Once strength or feeling in the legs was gone, the victim would be unable to push up in order to breathe, and death would occur quickly. That is why the Romans sometimes practiced *crucifracture*—the breaking of the legs below the knees—when they wanted to hasten the process (cf. John 19:31).

Dehydration, hypovolemic shock, and congestive heart failure sometimes hastened death as well. In Jesus' case, it seems likely that acute exhaustion was probably another major contributing factor.

THE HUMILIATION

Aside from the physical pain of crucifixion, the most notable feature of this type of execution was the stigma of disgrace that was attached to it. Victims were mercilessly taunted. They were usually hanged naked. They were deliberately made a spectacle of shame and reproach. Hebrews 12:2 refers to this when it says Christ "endured the cross, despising the shame."

Scripture indicates that Christ was deliberately stripped of all clothing and dignity when He was crucified. In fact, the soldiers who kept guard over Him gambled for what remained of His clothing. Matthew writes, "Then they crucified Him, and divided His garments, casting lots, that it might be fulfilled which was spoken by the prophet: 'They divided My garments among them, and for My clothing they cast lots.' Sitting down, they kept watch over Him there" (Matthew 27:35–36). The prophecy referred to is Psalm 22:18, which foretold the casting of lots for Jesus clothes. This, too, was part of God's sovereign plan from the beginning.

There may have been as many as five pieces of clothing for the soldiers to divide among themselves: sandals, a robelike garment, a headpiece, a belt, and a tunic. That was the traditional clothing for a Jewish man in Jesus' culture. Evidently the normal arrangement provided for the quaternion charged with guarding a victim to distribute his clothing equally among themselves. If each selected one garment, a fifth garment would remain. Thus according to John, "The soldiers, when they had crucified Jesus, took His garments and made four parts, to each soldier a part, and also the tunic. Now the tunic was without seam, woven from the top in one piece. They said therefore among themselves, "Let us not tear it, but cast lots for it, whose it shall be" (John 19:23–24). The tunic, a fine, woven outer garment, was undoubtedly the best of all the garments, and therefore it was the one they gambled for. Having divided His garments, they sat down to keep watch over Him.

Pilate added to the mockery by having a large placard erected over Jesus' head with the only actual indictment that had been brought against Him. "And they put up over His head the accusation written against Him: THIS IS JESUS THE KING OF THE JEWS" (Matthew 27:37).

Each of the gospel writers mentions the sign, but each gives a slightly different variation of what it said. Luke 23:38 and John 19:20 both say that the inscription was written in Greek, Latin, and Hebrew, so the variant readings are easily explained. Either they represent slightly different translations of the inscription, or (more likely) they are meant as elliptical restatements of the gist of the full inscription. All accounts agree that the inscription said THE KING OF THE JEWS (Matthew 27:37; Mark 15:26; Luke 23:38; John 19:19). Luke adds "THIS IS" at the beginning, and Matthew started with "THIS IS JESUS." John's version begins, "JESUS OF NAZARETH." Putting them all together, it appears the full inscription actually read, "THIS IS JESUS OF NAZARETH, THE KING OF THE JEWS."

John says the Sanhedrin was unhappy with that wording, and they wanted the indictment to read, *"He said, 'I am the King of the Jews'"* (John 19:21, emphasis added). But by then, Pilate was tired of playing minion to them, and he told them, "What I have written, I have written" (v. 22).

Christ was crucified between two thieves, and even they joined in the mockery aimed at Him. Matthew writes,

> Then two robbers were crucified with Him, one on the right and another on the left. And those who passed by blasphemed Him, wagging their heads and saying, "You who destroy the temple and build it in three days, save Yourself! If You are the Son of God, come down from the cross." Likewise the chief priests also, mocking with the scribes and elders, said, "He saved others; Himself He cannot save. If He is the King of Israel, let Him now come down from the cross, and we will believe Him. He trusted in God; let Him deliver Him now if He will have Him; for He said, 'I am the Son of God.'" Even the robbers who were crucified with Him reviled Him with the same thing. (Matthew 27:38–44)

The Greek term for "robbers" signifies that they were no petty thieves, but miscreants who lived as outlaws and brigands, leaving a path of destruction and human misery in their wake. They may well have been Barabbas's accomplices, and in that case, the cross on which Christ was crucified would have originally been intended for their leader (which would also mean that these robbers had been accomplices to murder as well as thievery).

In any case, it is clear that they were the cruelest sort of fellows, because while they hung on their own crosses, each in the throes of his own death agonies, they used what little strength was available to them to taunt Christ, who had never done them harm. They mocked Him for the sheer sport of it, which speaks volumes about their true character.

Meanwhile, multitudes were passing by the cross, also hurling insults at the Savior and wagging their heads (vv. 39–40). This was another fulfillment of the array of crucifixion prophecies contained in Psalm 22, where David prophetically describes the cross from the Messiah's own perspective:

> *I am a worm, and no man;*
> *A reproach of men, and despised by the people.*
> *All those who see Me ridicule Me;*
> *They shoot out the lip, they shake the head, saying,*
> *"He trusted in the* LORD, *let Him rescue Him;*
> *Let Him deliver Him, since He delights in Him!"*
>
> vv. 6–8

The mockers around the cross cited the same misunderstanding of Jesus' words in John 2:19 that the false witnesses had used in the trial before Caiaphas. He had said, "Destroy this temple, and in three days I will raise it up." But as John points out, "He was speaking of the temple of His body" (v. 21). Christ's enemies did not know the prophecy was about to come true, but they persisted in putting a wrong interpretation on His words, and that became the focus of their mockery.

The Sanhedrin was present as well, no doubt inciting much of the mockery. They had come out to the crucifixion site in order to gloat and witness the culmination of their evil plot before they went home to the sanctimonious observance of their Passover meals.

Their mockery was a desperate attempt to convince themselves and all other witnesses that Jesus was not Israel's Messiah. They believed the Messiah could not be conquered. The fact that Jesus hung there dying so helplessly was proof, as far as they were concerned, that He was not who He claimed to be. So they reveled in their triumph, strutting and swaggering among the crowd of observers, announcing to everyone, but to no one in particular, "He saved others; Himself He cannot save. If He is the King of Israel, let Him now come down from the cross, and we will believe Him. He trusted in God; let Him deliver Him now if He will have Him" (Matthew 27:42–43). If they had been the kind of spiritual leaders they were supposed to be, they should have noticed that their words were an almost verbatim fulfillment of the prophecy of Psalm 22:8.

They were the highest priests in Israel. They had everything to do with religion but nothing to do with God. They therefore bore the greatest guilt of all who participated in the humiliation of Christ. Although they pretended to sit in Moses' seat (Matthew 23:2), they did not believe Moses (John 5:46). Although they claimed to be spokesmen for God, they were actually children of Satan (John 8:44).

As always, Jesus did not revile those who reviled Him. Rather, His only words about His tormenters as He hung on the cross were a tender plea to God for mercy on their behalf (Luke 23:34). He had come to the cross willingly, knowingly, and in submissive obedience to God—to die for others' sins. And though the abuse and torture *men* heaped on Him were agony beyond our ability to fathom—those were nothing compared to the wrath of God against the sin He bore.

ENDNOTES

1 Frederick Farrar, *The Life of Christ* (New York: A. L. Burt, n.d.), 499.

2 "The Crucifixion of Jesus: The Passion of Christ from a Medical Point of View," *Arizona Medicine,* vol. 22, no. 3 (March 1965), 183–87.

11

Therefore My Father loves Me, because I lay down My life that I may take it again. No one takes it from Me, but I lay it down of Myself. I have power to lay it down, and I have power to take it again. This command I have received from My Father.

—JOHN 10:17–18

11

🔱 The Seven Last Sayings of Christ

BECAUSE OF THE PHYSICAL RIGORS of crucifixion, Christ spoke only with great difficulty during His final hours on the cross. Scripture records only seven brief sayings from the Savior on the cross, but every one of them reveals that Christ remained sovereignly in control, even as He died. And each of His sayings was rich with significance.

A PLEA FOR FORGIVENESS

The first was a plea for mercy on behalf of His tormentors. Luke records that shortly after the cross was raised on Calvary—while the soldiers were still gambling for His clothing, He prayed to God for forgiveness on their behalf: "And when they had come to the place called Calvary, there they crucified Him, and the criminals, one on the right hand and the other on the left. Then Jesus said, 'Father, forgive them, for they do not know what they do.'" (Luke 23:33–34).

J. C. Ryle wrote, "These words were probably spoken while

our Lord was being nailed to the cross, or as soon as the cross was reared up on end. It is worthy of remark that as soon as the blood of the Great Sacrifice began to flow, the Great High Priest began to intercede." While others were mocking Him—just as the taunting and jeering reached a fever pitch—Christ responded in precisely the opposite way most men would have. Instead of threatening, lashing back, or cursing His enemies, He prayed to God on their behalf.

As we have seen with so many of the details surrounding Jesus' death, this priestly intercession on behalf of His own killers was done in fulfillment of Old Testament prophecy: "He poured out His soul unto death, and He was numbered with the transgressors, and He bore the sin of many, *and made intercession for the transgressors*" (Isaiah 53:12, emphasis added). The whole meaning of the cross is summed up in this one act of intercession. "For God did not send His Son into the world to condemn the world, but that the world through Him might be saved" (John 3:17). Certainly any mortal man would have desired only to curse or revile his killers under these circumstances. One might even think that God incarnate would wish to call down some thunderous blast of judgment against men acting so wickedly. But Christ was on a mission of mercy. He was dying to purchase forgiveness for sins. And even at the very height of His agony, compassion was what filled his heart.

The phrase "for they do not know what they do" does not suggest that they were unaware that they were sinning. Ignorance does not absolve anyone from sin. These people were behaving wickedly, and they knew it. Most were fully aware of the *fact* of their wrongdoing. Pilate himself had testified of Jesus' innocence. The Sanhedrin was fully aware that no legitimate charges could be brought against Him. The soldiers and the crowd could easily see that a great injustice was being done, and yet they all gleefully participated. Many of the taunting spectators at Calvary had heard Christ teach and seen

Him do miracles. They could not have really believed in their hearts that He deserved to die this way. Their ignorance itself was inexcusable, and it certainly did not absolve them of guilt for what they were doing.

But they were ignorant of the *enormity* of their crime. They were blinded to the full reality that they were crucifying God the Son. They were spiritually insensitive, because they loved darkness rather than light. Therefore they did not recognize that the One they were putting to death was the Light of the World. "Had they known, they would not have crucified the Lord of glory" (1 Corinthians 2:8).

How was Jesus' prayer answered? In innumerable ways. The first answer came with the conversion of one of the thieves on the cross next to Jesus (Luke 23:40–43). Another followed immediately, with the conversion of a centurion, one of the soldiers who had crucified Christ (v. 47). Other answers to the prayer came in the weeks and months that followed the crucifixion—particularly at Pentecost—as untold numbers of people in Jerusalem were converted to Christ. No doubt many of them were the same people who had clamored for Jesus' death and railed at Him from the foot of the cross. We're told in Acts 6:7, for example, that a great number of the temple priests later confessed Jesus as Lord.

It is important to understand that Jesus' plea for his killers' forgiveness did not guarantee the immediate and unconditional forgiveness of everyone who participated in the crucifixion. He was interceding on behalf of all who would repent and turn to Him as Lord and Savior. His prayer was that when they finally realized the enormity of what they had done and sought the heavenly Father's forgiveness for their sin, He would not hold the murder of His beloved Son against them. Divine forgiveness is never granted to people who remain in unbelief and sin. Those who clung to their hatred of Jesus were by no means automatically absolved from their crime by

Jesus' prayer. But those who repented and sought forgiveness, like the centurion, or the thief on the cross, or the priests, or the people in the crowd—all who later embraced Him would find abundant mercy in answer to Christ's petition on their behalf.

The prayer was a token of mercy offered to all who heard. He prayed aloud for their sakes (cf. John 11:42). Their sin was so unfathomably heinous that if witnesses had not actually heard Him pray for His killers' forgiveness, most might have assumed they had committed an unpardonable offense.

The forgiveness Christ prayed for is freely offered to all (Revelation 22:17) In fact, God is *eager* to forgive repentant sinners. (The Prodigal Son's father pictures God's eagerness to forgive.) He pleads for every sinner to be reconciled to Him (2 Corinthians 5:20; Ezekiel 18:3–32; Acts 17:30). Those who do, He promises to lavish freely with forgiveness. And that offer was extended even to those who personally participated in the murder of Jesus.

A PROMISE OF SALVATION

Christ's second utterance from the cross marks the first glorious fulfillment of His prayer for His killers' forgiveness, and it shows how generously that forgiveness was bestowed, even on the most unlikely of recipients.

As the hours of agony passed on the cross, one of the two thieves who had mocked Christ earlier now had a change of heart. What prompted the change is not mentioned. Perhaps the thief heard and was touched by Jesus' prayer for mercy, realizing that it applied to him. Whatever prompted his turnaround, it was a tremendous miracle.

The man was undoubtedly one of the most thoroughly degenerate people on the scene. He and his confederate were career criminals, men whose lives had been devoted to thievery and mayhem. The deep-down bad-to-the-bone wickedness of their character was shown by the fact that they used their dying strength to join in the taunting of Christ. They obviously knew of His innocence, because the repentant thief finally rebuked his cohort, saying, "This Man has done nothing wrong" (Luke 23:41). Yet until one of them repented, they both were heaping ridicule and scorn on Him anyway.

But there came a point when one thief's taunting turned to silence, and the silence turned to repentance, and the thief's heart was utterly changed. As he studied Jesus, suffering all that abuse so patiently—never reviling or insulting His tormentors—the thief began to see that this Man on the center cross was indeed who He claimed to be. The proof of his repentance is seen in his immediate change of behavior, as his derisive insults turned to words of praise for Christ.

First he rebuked his partner in crime: "Do you not even fear God, seeing you are under the same condemnation? And we indeed justly, for we receive the due reward of our deeds; but this Man has done nothing wrong" (vv. 40–41). In saying that much, he confessed his own guilt, and he also acknowledged the justice of the penalty he had been given. He affirmed the innocence of Christ as well.

Then he turned to Jesus and confessed Him as Lord: "Lord, remember me when You come into Your kingdom" (v. 42).

That confession of Jesus as Lord and King was immediately followed by the second of Jesus' seven last sayings: "And Jesus said to him, 'Assuredly, I say to you, today you will be with Me in Paradise'" (v. 43).

No sinner was ever given more explicit assurance of salvation. This most unlikely of saints was received immediately and unconditionally into the Savior's kingdom. The incident is one of the greatest biblical illustrations of the truth of justification by faith. This man had done nothing to *merit* salvation. Indeed, he was in no position to do anything meritorious. Already gasping in the throes of his own death agonies, he had no hope of ever *earning* Christ's favor. But realizing that he was in an utterly hopeless situation, the thief sought only a modest token of mercy from Christ: "Remember me."

His request was a final, desperate, end-of-his-rope plea for a small mercy he knew he did not deserve. It echoes the plaintive cry of the publican, who "would not so much as raise his eyes to heaven, but beat his breast, saying, 'God, be merciful to me a sinner!'" (Luke 18:13). For either man to be granted eternal life and received into the kingdom, it had to be on the merits of Another. And yet in both cases, Jesus gave full and immediate assurance of complete forgiveness and eternal life. Those are classic proofs that justification is by faith alone.

Jesus' words to the dying thief conveyed to him an unqualified promise of full forgiveness, covering every evil deed he had ever done. He wasn't expected to atone for his own sins, do penance, or perform any ritual. He wasn't consigned to purgatory—though if there really were such a place, and if the doctrines that invariably accompany belief in purgatory were true, this man would have been assured a long stay there. But instead, his forgiveness was full, and free, and immediate: "*Today* you will be with Me in Paradise."

That was all Christ said to him. But it was all the thief needed to hear. He was still suffering unspeakable physical torment, but the misery in his soul was now gone. For the first time in his life, he was free from the burden of his sin. The Savior, at his side, was bearing that sin for him. And the thief was now clothed in Christ's perfect righteousness. Soon they would be in Paradise together. The thief had Christ's own word on it.

A PROVISION FOR HIS MOTHER

Jesus' enemies were not the only spectators at the cross. As word got around Jerusalem that morning that Christ was under arrest and had been condemned to death by the Sanhedrin, some of His closest loved ones came to be near Him. John 19:25 describes the scene: "Now there stood by the cross of Jesus His mother, and His mother's sister, Mary the wife of Clopas, and Mary Magdalene." Some interpreters believe John mentions only three women, and that "His mother's sister" is the same person as "Mary the wife of Clopas." But that would mean these two sisters were both named Mary, and that seems highly unlikely. Instead, it seems John was saying there were three women named Mary present (Jesus' mother, Mrs. Clopas, and Mary Magdalene), as well as a fourth woman (Mary's sister) whose name is not given—but she might have been Salome, the mother of James and John. John also indicates in verse 26 that he himself was present, referring to himself the way he always did in his Gospel, as "the disciple whom [Jesus] loved" (cf. John 21:20–24).

The pain of watching Jesus die must have been agonizing for Jesus' loved ones. But for no one was it more difficult than Mary, His earthly mother. Years before, at His birth, the elderly prophet Simeon had told her, "Behold, this Child is destined for the fall and rising of many in Israel, and for a sign which will be spoken against (*yes, a sword will pierce through your own soul also*), that the thoughts of many hearts may be revealed" (Luke 2:34–35, emphasis added). The sword Simeon spoke of was now piercing her heart, as she watched her firstborn Son die.

She had reared Him from childhood. She knew His utter perfection better than anyone. And yet as she watched, crowds of people poured contempt on her Son, cruelly mocking and abusing Him. His bleeding, emaciated form hung helplessly on the cross, and all she could do was watch His agony. The sorrow and pain such a sight would cause His mother is unfathomable. And yet instead of shrieking and crumpling in hysteria, turning and fleeing in terror, or falling into a faint at the horrible sight, she stood. She is the very model of courage.

Jesus saw her standing and grieving there, and His third saying from the cross reflects the tender love of a Son for His mother. "When Jesus therefore saw His mother, and the disciple whom He loved standing by, He said to His mother, 'Woman, behold your son!' Then He said to the disciple, 'Behold your mother!' And from that hour that disciple took her to his own home" (John 19:26–27). When Jesus said, "Behold your son," He was not referring to Himself. He probably nodded at John. He was making a gracious provision for Mary in the years to come. He was delegating to John the responsibility to care for Mary in her old age.

This was a beautiful gesture, and it says a lot about the personal nature of Jesus' love. Although He was dying under the most excruciating kind of anguish, Jesus, the King of love, selflessly turned aside to care for the earthly needs of those who stood by His side. Although He was occupied with the most important event in the history of redemption, He remembered to make provision for the needs of one woman, His mother.

He addresses her as "woman." Nowhere in the Gospels does He ever call her "mother"; only "woman." The expression conveys no disrespect. But it does underscore the fact that Christ was much more to Mary than a Son. He was her *Savior,* too (cf. Luke 1:47). Mary was no sinless co-redemptrix. She was as dependent on divine grace as the lowliest of sinners, and after Christ reached adulthood, her relationship to Him was the same as that of any obedient believer to the Lord. She was a disciple; He was the Master.

Christ Himself rebuked those who wanted to elevate Mary to a place of extraordinary veneration: "A certain woman from the crowd raised her voice and said to Him, 'Blessed is the womb that bore You, and the breasts which nursed You!' But He said, 'More than that, blessed are those who hear the word of God and keep it!'"(Luke 11:27–28). Mary was blessed because she was obedient to the Word of God—the same as any other believer. Her position as Christ's mother did not carry with it any special titles such as comediatrix, queen of heaven, or any of the other forms of deification medieval superstition has attached to the popular concept of Mary.

Let's be perfectly clear: It is a form of idolatry to bestow on Mary honor, titles, or attributes that in effect give her a coequal status in the redemptive work of her Son or elevate her as a special object of veneration.

Nonetheless, Christ loved and honored His mother *as a mother*. He fulfilled the fifth commandment as perfectly as He fulfilled them all. And part of the responsibility of honoring one's parents is the duty to see that they are cared for in their old age. Christ did not neglect that duty.

It is perhaps significant that Jesus did not commit Mary to the care of His own half-brothers. Mary was evidently a widow by now. Nothing is said of Joseph after the gospel narratives about Jesus' birth and childhood. Apparently he had died by the time Jesus began His public ministry. But Scripture suggests that after Jesus' birth Mary and Joseph had a marital relationship that was in every sense normal (Matthew 1:25). Despite the claims of the Roman Catholic Church, Scripture does not allow us to believe Mary remained perpetually a virgin. On the contrary, the gospels clearly state that Jesus had brothers (Mark 3:31–35; John 2:12; Luke 8:19–21). Matthew even names them: "James, Joses, Simon, and Judas" (Matthew 13:55). They would have in fact been half-brothers, as the natural offspring of Mary and Joseph.

Why didn't Jesus appoint one of His own brothers to look after Mary? Because, according to John 7:5, "His brothers did not believe in Him." They *became* believers when Jesus rose from the dead, and therefore Acts 1:14 records that they were among the group meeting for prayer in the Upper Room when the Holy Spirit came at Pentecost: "These all continued with one accord in prayer and supplication, with the women and Mary the mother of Jesus, *and with His brothers*" (emphasis added). But they were evidently not believers yet when Jesus died. So as He was dying on the cross, He committed His mother to the care of His beloved disciple, John.

A PETITION TO THE FATHER

Christ's fourth saying from the cross is by far the richest with mystery and meaning. Matthew writes, "Now from the sixth hour until the ninth hour there was darkness over all the land. And about the ninth hour Jesus cried out with a loud voice, saying, 'Eli, Eli, lama sabachthani?' that is, 'My God, My God, why have You forsaken Me?'" (Matthew 27:45–46).

It might seem at first glance that Christ was merely reciting the words of Psalm 22:1 ("My God, My God, why have You forsaken Me? Why are You so far from helping Me, and from the words of My groaning?"). But given the fact that all of Psalm 22 is an extended prophecy about the crucifixion, it might be better to see the psalm as a prophetic anticipation of the cry of Jesus' heart as He bore the sins of the world on the cross. It was no mere recitation.

Some commentators have gone to great lengths to explain why Jesus would utter such words. To them, it seems unthinkable that Jesus would actually feel abandoned on the cross—and even more unthinkable to surmise that God in any sense abandoned His beloved Son. And so they insist that Jesus was merely reciting Scripture, not expressing what He truly felt in His heart.

But that betrays a serious misunderstanding of what was taking place on the cross. As Christ hung there, He was bearing the sins of the world. He was dying as a substitute for others. To Him was imputed the guilt of their sins, and He was suffering the punishment for those sins on their behalf. And the very essence of that punishment was the outpouring of God's wrath against sinners. In some mysterious way during those awful hours on the cross, the Father poured out the full measure of His wrath against sin, and the recipient of that wrath was God's own beloved Son!

In this lies the true meaning of the cross. Those who try to explain the atoning work of Christ in any other terms inevitably end up nullifying the truth of Christ's atonement altogether. Christ was not merely providing an example for us to follow. He was no mere martyr being sacrificed to the wickedness of the men who crucified Him. He wasn't merely making a public display so that people would see the awfulness of sin. He wasn't offering a ransom price to Satan—or any of the other various explanations religious liberals, cultists, and pseudo-Christian religionists have tried to suggest over the years.

Here's what was happening on the cross: God was punishing His own Son as if He had committed every wicked deed done by every sinner who would ever believe. And He did it so that He could forgive and treat those redeemed ones as if they had lived Christ's perfect life of righteousness.

Scripture teaches this explicitly: "He made Him who knew no sin to be sin for us, that we might become the righteousness of God in Him" (2 Corinthians 5:21). "Surely He has borne our griefs and carried our sorrows; yet we esteemed Him stricken, smitten by God, and afflicted. But He was wounded for our transgressions, He was bruised for our iniquities; the chastisement for our peace was upon Him, and by His stripes we are healed" (Isaiah 53:4–5). "He had done no violence, nor was any deceit in His mouth. Yet it pleased the LORD to bruise Him; He has put Him to grief . . . [in order to] make His soul an offering for sin" (vv. 9–10). "Messiah shall be cut off, but not for Himself" (Daniel 9:26). "What the law could not do in that it was weak through the flesh, God did by sending His own Son in the likeness of sinful flesh, on account of sin: He condemned sin in the flesh" (Romans 8:3). "Christ has redeemed us from the curse of the law, having become a curse for us (for it is written, 'Cursed is everyone who hangs on a tree')" (Galatians 3:13). "Christ also suffered once for sins, the just for the unjust, that He might bring us to God, being put to death in the flesh" (1 Peter 3:18). "He Himself is the propitiation for our sins" (1 John 2:2).

That word *propitiation* speaks of an offering made to satisfy God. Christ's death was a satisfaction rendered to God on behalf of those whom He redeemed. "It *pleased* the LORD to bruise Him" (Isaiah 53:10, emphasis added). God the Father saw the travail of His Son's soul, and He was *satisfied* (v. 11). Christ made propitiation by shedding His blood (Romans 3:25; Hebrews 2:17).

It was God's own wrath against sin, God's own righteousness, and God's own sense of justice that Christ satisfied on the cross. The shedding of His blood was a sin offering rendered to God. His death was *not* merely a satisfaction of public justice, nor was it a ransom paid to Satan. Neither Satan nor anyone else had any right to claim a ransom from God for sinners. But when Christ ransomed the elect from sin (1 Timothy 2:6), the ransom price was paid to God. Christ died in our place and in our stead—and He received the very same outpouring of divine wrath in all its fury that *we* deserved for our sin. It was a punishment so severe that a mortal man could spend all eternity in the torments of hell, and still he would not have begun to exhaust the divine wrath that was heaped on Christ at the cross.

This was the true measure of Christ's sufferings on the cross. The physical pains of crucifixion—dreadful as they were—were nothing compared to the wrath of the Father against Him. The anticipation of *this* was what had caused Him to sweat blood in the garden. This was why He had looked ahead to the cross with such horror. We cannot begin to fathom all that was involved in paying the price of our sin. It's sufficient to understand that all our worst fears about the horrors of hell—and more—were realized by Him as He received the due penalty of others' wrongdoing.

And in that awful, sacred hour, it was as if the Father abandoned Him. Though there was surely no interruption in the Father's love for Him *as a Son,* God nonetheless turned away from Him and forsook Him *as our Substitute.*

The fact that Christ—suffering from exhaustion, blood loss, asphyxia, and all the physical anguish of the cross—nonetheless made this cry "with a loud voice" proves it was no mere recitation of a psalm. This was the outcry of His soul; it was the very thing the psalm foretold. And as we shall see in the chapter that follows, all nature groaned with Him.

A PLEADING FOR RELIEF

"After this, Jesus, knowing that all things were now accomplished, that the Scripture might be fulfilled, said, 'I thirst!'" (John 19:28). This was Christ's fifth utterance from the cross. As the end neared, Christ uttered a final plea for physical relief. Earlier He had spat out the vinegar mixed with painkiller that had been offered Him. Now, when He asked for relief from the horrible thirst of dehydration, He was given only a sponge saturated with pure vinegar. John writes, "Now a vessel full of sour wine was sitting there; and they filled a sponge with sour wine, put it on hyssop, and put it to His mouth" (v. 29).

In His thirst we see the true humanity of Christ. Although He was God incarnate, in His physical body, He experienced all the normal human limitations of real human flesh. And none was more vivid than this moment of agonizing thirst after hours of hanging on the cross. He suffered bodily to an extent few have ever suffered. And—again, so that the Scriptures might be fulfilled—all He was given to salve His fiery thirst was vinegar. "They also gave me gall for my food, and for my thirst they gave me vinegar to drink" (Psalm 69:21).

A PROCLAMATION OF VICTORY

John's account of the crucifixion continues: "So when Jesus had received the sour wine, He said, "It is finished!" (John 19:30). In the Greek text, this sixth utterance of Jesus from the cross is a single word: *Tetelestai!* Luke 23:46 indicates He made this cry "with a loud voice."

It was a triumphant outcry, full of rich meaning. He did not mean merely that His earthly life was over. He meant that the work the Father had given Him to do was now complete. As He hung there, looking every bit like a pathetic, wasted victim, He nonetheless celebrated the greatest triumph in the history of the universe. Christ's atoning work was finished; redemption for sinners was complete; and He was triumphant.

Christ had fulfilled on behalf of sinners everything the law of God required of them. Full atonement had been made. Everything the ceremonial law foreshadowed had been accomplished. God's justice was satisfied. The ransom for sin was paid in full. The wages of sin were settled forever. All that remained was for Christ to die so that He might rise again.

That is why nothing can be added to the work of Christ for salvation. No religious ritual—neither baptism, nor penance, nor any other human work—needs to be added to make His work effectual. No supplemental human works could ever augment or improve the atonement He purchased on the cross. The sinner is required to contribute nothing to earn forgiveness or a right standing with God; the merit of Christ alone is sufficient for our full salvation. *Tetelestai!* His atoning work is done. All of it. "For by grace you have been saved through faith, and that not of yourselves; it is the gift of God, not of works, lest anyone should boast" (Ephesians 2:8–9).

A PRAYER OF CONSUMMATION

Christ's final saying from the cross, right after "It is finished!" was a prayer that expressed the unqualified submission that had been in His heart from the very beginning. Luke records those final words: "And when Jesus had cried out with a loud voice, He said, 'Father, "into Your hands I commit My spirit."' Having said this, He breathed His last" (Luke 23:46).

Christ died as no other man has ever died. In one sense He was murdered by the hands of wicked men (Acts 2:23). In another sense it was the Father who sent Him to the cross and bruised Him there, putting Him to grief—and it pleased the Father to do so (Isaiah 53:10). Yet in still another sense, no one took Christ's life. He gave it up willingly for those whom He loved (John 10:17–18).

When He finally expired on the cross, it was not with a wrenching struggle against His killers. He did not display any frenzied death throes. His final passage into death—like every other aspect of the crucifixion drama—was a deliberate act of His own sovereign will, showing that to the very end, He was sovereignly in control of all that was happening. John says, "Bowing His head, He gave up His spirit" (John 19:30). Quietly, submissively, He simply yielded up His life.

Everything had come to pass exactly as He said it would. Not only Jesus, but also His killers, and the mocking crowd, together with Pilate, Herod, and the Sanhedrin—all had perfectly fulfilled the determined purpose and foreknowledge of God to the letter.

And thus Christ calmly and majestically displayed His utter sovereignty to the end. It seemed to all who loved Him—and even many who cared little for Him—like a supreme tragedy. But it was the greatest moment of victory in the history of redemption, and Christ would make that fact gloriously clear when He burst triumphantly from the grave just days later.

12

Truly this was the Son of God!

—MATTHEW 27:54

12

❧ All Creation Groans

SCRIPTURE RECORDS a number of supernatural phenomena that occurred while Jesus hung on the cross. Those events constituted God's own supernatural commentary on the cross. They are further proof of the extraordinary importance of what was occurring that day just outside Jerusalem.

The routes to the city that day were jammed with pilgrims coming and going as they prepared to celebrate Passover. Few if any of them realized the vital truth that God's true Paschal Lamb was dying that very day to provide forgiveness for all the sins of all the saints of all time. It was the very focal point of redemptive history, and yet as far as Jerusalem was concerned on that day, relatively few were taking notice. And few who witnessed the murder of Jesus had any idea of what was really taking place.

But then suddenly all nature seemed to stop and pay attention.

THE SUN DARKENED

The first of the miraculous signs that accompanied Jesus' death was the darkening of the sky. Matthew writes, "Now from the sixth hour until the ninth hour there was darkness over all the land" (Matthew 27:45). Matthew was counting hours in accord with the Jewish system, so the sixth hour would have been noon. At the moment the noon sun should have been brightest in the sky, a darkness fell over all the land, and remained for three hours.

This was probably not a total blackness, but rather a severe darkening of the normal daylight intensity of the sun. "Over all the land" is an expression that might refer to the land of Israel, or it could refer to the whole world. I'm inclined to think that the sun itself was dimmed, so that the darkness would have been universal, and not limited to the local area surrounding Jerusalem.

It could not have been an eclipse, because Passover always fell on a full moon, and a solar eclipse would be out of the question during the full moon. God is certainly able to dim the sun's light. During Moses' time, darkness fell on Egypt because the plague of locusts was so thick that the flying insects blocked the sunlight (Exodus 10:14–15). In Joshua's time the opposite occurred, and the sun seemed to stand still over Israel for a whole twenty-four-hour period (Joshua 10:12–14). In Hezekiah's day, the shadows turned backward ten degrees, as the earth's rotation seemed to reverse for about forty minutes (2 Kings 20:9–11). The darkening of the sun is commonly mentioned in Scripture as an apocalyptic sign (Isaiah 50:3; Joel 2:31; Revelation 9:2). Amos wrote of the last days of the earth, "'And it shall come to pass in that day,' says the Lord GOD, 'that I will make the sun go down at noon, and I will darken the earth in broad daylight'" (Amos 8:9).

According to some of the church fathers, the supernatural darkness that accompanied the crucifixion was noticed throughout the world at the time. Tertullian mentioned this event in his *Apologeticum*—a defense of Christianity written to pagan skeptics: "At the moment of Christ's death, the light departed from the sun, and the land was darkened at noonday, which wonder is related in your own annals and is preserved in your archives to this day."

Throughout Scripture, darkness is connected with judgment, and supernatural darkness of this type signifies cataclysmic doom (cf. Isaiah 5:30; Joel 2:2; Amos 5:20; Zephaniah 1:14–15). Various interpreters have explained this darkness several ways. Some have suggested God sent it as a veil to cover the sufferings and nakedness of His Son, as an act of mercy toward Christ. Others have suggested it signified His displeasure with those who put Christ to death. Scripture does not say *why* the darkness; it only reports it as a fact. The darkness clearly does seem to signify divine judgment, and coming as it did during the time when Christ's suffering was most intense, in the three hours before He cried out, "My God, My God, why have You forsaken Me?" (Matthew 27:46)—it may well signify the Father's judgment falling on Christ as He bore in His person our guilt.

In any case, the darkness is certainly an appropriate reminder that the cross was a place of judgment, and in those awful hours of darkness, Christ was standing in our place as the wrath of God was being poured upon Him for our transgressions. And that may well be why the biblical narrative links the culmination of the darkness with Christ's outcry to the Father: "And about the ninth hour Jesus cried out with a loud voice, saying, 'Eli, Eli, lama sabachthani?' that is, 'My God, My God, why have You forsaken Me?' Some of those who stood there, when they heard that, said, 'This Man is calling for Elijah!'" (vv. 46–47).

Eli is Hebrew for God. (Mark uses the Aramaic cognate, *Eloi*.) *Lama sabachthani* is Aramaic, meaning, "Why have You forsaken Me?" Since Aramaic was the common language of the region, it seems unlikely that all the spectators at the cross were truly ignorant about the meaning of His words. Thus their remark ("This

Man is calling for Elijah!") was a deliberate misrepresentation of His words—another cruel and sadistic sneer at Christ.

Their behavior makes clear their mocking intent: "Immediately one of them ran and took a sponge, filled it with sour wine and put it on a reed, and offered it to Him to drink. The rest said, 'Let Him alone; let us see if Elijah will come to save Him'" (vv. 47–49). The one who ran to fetch the vinegar obviously did so for melodramatic effect, to complete his mockery by pretending to be generous and compassionate to Jesus, but really only seeking another means to taunt. Vinegar would have been a disappointing refreshment to someone in such a state of dehydration—though it would have helped some.

In fact, shortly after this, when Christ did utter the words, "I thirst" (John 19:28), the vinegar was all He was offered. By then it was close at hand (v. 29) because of this individual's devilish taunt. But at this point, other bystanders forbade the prankster from giving Christ even mock assistance, saying, "Let Him alone; let us see if Elijah will come to save Him." Despite the ominous darkness, they were reveling in Christ's sufferings, and they did not want anyone to offer Him relief—even if the assistance rendered was merely a fiendish insult.

Matthew indicates that the taunting continued to the very end. It was at some point in the midst of that continued taunting that Christ said, "I thirst," and was then given a sponge full of vinegar. Shortly afterward, "Jesus cried out again with a loud voice"—saying "Telelestai!" then audibly giving Himself to God—He "yielded up His spirit" (Matthew 27:50).

THE VEIL TORN

At the moment of Christ's death, a series of remarkable miracles occurred. Matthew writes, "Then, behold, the veil of the temple was torn in two from top to bottom" (v. 51).

The veil was a heavy curtain that blocked the entrance to the Holy of Holies in the Jerusalem temple, the place where the Ark of the Covenant was kept, symbolizing the sacred presence of God. Josephus described the veil as ornately decorated, made of blue woven fabric.

Only one person ever traversed the veil, and that was the high priest. He entered the Holy of Holies only once a year, on the Day of Atonement, with the blood of a sacrifice. The veil was of vital symbolic importance, signifying "that the way into the Holiest of All was not yet made manifest" (Hebrews 9:8). In other words, it was a constant reminder that sin renders humanity unfit for the presence of God. The fact that the sin offering was offered annually—and countless other sacrifices repeated daily—showed that sin could not truly and permanently be atoned for or erased by animal sacrifices. "For it is not possible that the blood of bulls and goats could take away sins" (Hebrews 10:4).

"But Christ came as High Priest of the good things to come, with the greater and more perfect tabernacle not made with hands, that is, not of this creation. Not with the blood of goats and calves, but with His own blood He entered the Most Holy Place once for all, having obtained eternal redemption" (Hebrews 9:11–12). The tearing of the curtain at the moment of Jesus' death dramatically symbolized that His sacrifice was a sufficient atonement for sins forever, and the way into the Holy of Holies was now open. In effect, the entire Levitical system of rituals, animal sacrifices—even the priesthood itself—were done away in the moment of His death. The redeemed now had free and direct access to the throne of grace without the need for priest or ritual (cf. Hebrews 4:16).

The tearing of the high curtain from top to bottom signified that it was God Himself who removed the barrier. He was in effect saying, "My Son has removed this veil and eliminated the need for it, through a single, perfect, once-for-all sacrifice that cleanses the redeemed from their sins forever. The way into My holy presence is now open to every believer and the access is free and unobstructed."

At the moment the tearing of the veil occurred, the temple was packed with worshipers who were there for the killing of their Passover lambs. By God's design, it was in the very hour that those thousands of lambs were being slain that the true Passover Lamb died. He was the real Lamb whom all the others merely symbolized. In fact, He perfectly fulfilled *all* the symbolism of the worship in the temple. From that day on, all the temple ceremonies lost their significance, because what they were meant to foreshadow had finally arrived. Within forty years, the temple itself would be completely destroyed when Titus sacked Jerusalem. But the true end of the Old Testament sacrificial system did not occur with the destruction of the temple in A.D. 70. It ended here at the moment of Jesus' death, when God sovereignly declared Christ's death a sufficient sacrifice for sins forever, by supernaturally splitting the temple veil from top to bottom and opening the way into His presence.

THE EARTH SHAKEN

Another miracle also occurred at the exact moment of Christ's death. "And the earth quaked, and the rocks were split" (Matthew 27:51). An earthquake powerful enough to split rocks would be a significant tremor. (The crowd in the temple probably assumed the earthquake was the cause of the tearing of the veil.) Such a powerful quake would be a frightening experience for everyone in the region of Judea. Although earthquakes were a fairly common phenomenon, an earthquake with enough force to split rocks would have instantly brought the entire city of Jerusalem to a halt for several minutes.

Earthquakes in Scripture are often used—like darkness—to signify a graphic display of divine judgment. In particular, earthquakes signify God's wrath. When Moses met with God at Sinai to receive the tablets of the law, "the whole mountain quaked greatly" (Exodus 19:18). David wrote, "Then the earth shook and trembled; the foundations of the hills also quaked and were shaken, because He was angry" (Psalm 18:7). "The earth shook; the heavens also dropped rain at the presence of God; Sinai itself was moved at the presence of God, the God of Israel" (Psalm 68:8). The prophet Nahum wrote,

> The LORD is slow to anger and great in power,
> And will not at all acquit the wicked.
> The LORD has His way
> In the whirlwind and in the storm,
> And the clouds are the dust of His feet.
> He rebukes the sea and makes it dry,
> And dries up all the rivers.
> Bashan and Carmel wither,
> And the flower of Lebanon wilts.
> The mountains quake before Him,
> The hills melt,
> And the earth heaves at His presence,
> Yes, the world and all who dwell in it.

NAHUM 1:3–5

The Book of Revelation indicates that the final judgment of the earth will commence with a global earthquake more powerful than any ever experienced (see Hebrews 12:26–27; Revelation 6:14–15).

So it is clear that a supernatural earthquake like this one could only signify the wrath of God. At the Cross, the wrath of God against sin was poured out on God's own Son. The accompanying earthquake, coming at the culminating moment of Christ's atoning work, was a kind of divine punctuation mark, perhaps signifying God's anger at the fact that sin had cost His Son so much.

THE DEAD RAISED

At that very same moment when Christ died, yet another miracle occurred: "The graves were opened; and many bodies of the saints who had fallen asleep were raised; and coming out of the graves after His resurrection, they went into the holy city and appeared to many" (Matthew 27:52–53).

Many of the tombs in and around Jerusalem to this day are hollow stone sepulchers, resting at ground level or just above. The earthquake was evidently powerful enough to split sepulchers like these. That was not the miracle; that might have occurred in any earthquake. The great miracle is that those who emerged from the broken sepulchers were raised from the dead.

Of all the Gospel writers, only Matthew mentions this event. Some have cited this as a reason to discount Matthew's veracity, suggesting that if such an event occurred, it would have certainly been noteworthy enough to catch the attention of all Jerusalem. But there's no reason to think this miracle was designed to capture people's attention. It seems to have been a remarkably quiet miracle, despite its spectacular nature.

Although *"many . . . saints who had fallen asleep"* were raised, not all were. These were select representatives of the multitude of saints buried in and around Jerusalem. The number raised is not specified, but the term "many" in this case could refer to as few as a dozen—or even fewer. (That would still be "many," given the fact that what Matthew is describing is people who were released from stone sarcophagi and came alive!) Still, despite the spectacular nature of the miracle itself, this seems to have been a fairly low-key event.

Notice, in fact, that those who rose from the dead did not appear in Jerusalem until after Jesus' resurrection. (The proper phrasing and punctuation of the verse is probably best reflected in the NIV translation: "They came out of the tombs, and after Jesus' resurrection they went into the holy city and appeared to many people.") Where these resurrected saints were in the days after they were loosed from the grave and before they appeared in Jerusalem is not specified. But the fact that they waited until after Christ's resurrection to appear to anyone reminds us that He is the firstfruits of those risen from the dead (1 Corinthians 15:20).

These risen saints most likely came forth from the dead in glorified bodies already fit for heaven (rather than being restored to life in unglorified mortal bodies, as Lazarus had been). They "appeared to many" (Matthew 27:53). Again, *how many* is not specified, but evidently there were enough eyewitnesses to verify the miracle. When Matthew wrote his Gospel, some of the eyewitnesses would have still been alive. Matthew doesn't say what became of the risen saints, but they undoubtedly ascended to glory not long after Jesus' resurrection.

Their appearance proved that Christ had conquered death, not merely for Himself, but for all the saints. One day *"all* who are in the graves will hear His voice and come forth" (John 5:28–29, emphasis added). This miraculous event prefigured that final great resurrection.

THE CENTURION SAVED

But perhaps the most important miracle that occurred at the moment of Jesus' death was the conversion of the centurion charged with overseeing the crucifixion. As Christ's atoning work was brought to completion, its dramatic saving power was already at work in the lives of those who were physically closest to Him. Matthew 27:54 says,

"So when the centurion and those with him, who were guarding Jesus, saw the earthquake and the things that had happened, they feared greatly, saying, 'Truly this was the Son of God!'"

A Roman centurion was the commander of a hundred-man division (or a "century")—the basic building block of a Roman legion. There were about twenty-five legions in the entire Roman army worldwide. Each legion comprised six thousand men, divided into ten cohorts of six hundred men each. Each cohort had three maniples, and each maniple was divided into two centuries. Each century was commanded by a centurion. The centurions were usually career officers, hardened men of war.

Because this particular officer was with those guarding Jesus, it appears he is the very one who had been given charge of overseeing and carrying out the crucifixion of Christ—and probably the crucifixions of the two thieves as well. He and his men were close eyewitnesses to everything that had happened since Jesus was taken to the Praetorium. They had personally kept Him under guard from that point on. (It is even possible that the centurion and some of the men with him were also the same soldiers who arrested Jesus the night before. If so, they had been eyewitnesses from the very beginning of the entire ordeal.) They had seen how Jesus held His silence while His enemies hurled accusations at Him. These same soldiers had strapped him to a post for the scourging, and watched while He suffered even that horrific beating with quiet grace and majesty. They themselves had mercilessly taunted Him, dressing Him in a faded soldier's tunic, pretending it was a royal robe. They had battered His head with a reed they gave Him as a mock scepter. These very same soldiers had also woven a crown of cruel thorns and mashed it into the skin of His scalp. They had spat on Him and taunted Him and mistreated Him in every conceivable fashion—and they had seen Him endure all those tortures without cursing or threatening any of His tormentors.

In all likelihood, the soldiers heard with their own ears when Pilate repeatedly declared Jesus' innocence. They knew very well that He was guilty of no crime that made Him a threat to Rome's interests. They must have been utterly amazed from the very beginning about how different He was from the typical criminal who was crucified. At first, they probably were inclined to write Him off as a madman. But by now they could see that He was not insane. He fit no category they had ever seen in the hundreds of crucifixions they had probably superintended.

Until now, the uniqueness of Christ had made no apparent impact whatsoever on these soldiers. They were hardened men, and Jesus' passivity made no difference in the way they treated Him. His obvious innocence had not gained any sympathy from them. They had showed Him no mercy. They were professional soldiers, trained to follow orders. And so they had dutifully nailed Jesus' hands and feet to the cross. They had set the cross upright and dropped it into the hole dug for it. They had cast lots for Jesus' garments. And then they had sat down to watch Him die.

But Christ's death was unlike any crucifixion they had ever witnessed. They heard Him pray for His killers. They saw the noble way He suffered. They heard when He cried out to His Father. They experienced three full hours of supernatural darkness. And when that darkness was followed by an earthquake at the very moment of Christ's death, the soldiers could no longer ignore the fact that Christ was indeed the Son of God.

Mark suggests that there was something about the way Jesus cried out that struck the centurion as supernatural—perhaps the powerful volume of His cry, coming from someone in such a weakened condition. Mark writes, "When the centurion, who stood opposite Him, saw that He cried out like this and breathed His last, he said, 'Truly this Man was the Son of God!'" (Mark 15:39).

Matthew indicates that it was also the earthquake, coming at the exact moment of Jesus' final outcry, that finally convinced the centurion and his soldiers that Jesus was the Son of God: "When [they] saw the earthquake and the things that had happened, they feared greatly" (Matthew 27:54).

Notice that Matthew indicates all the soldiers had the same reaction. When the earthquake occurred they "feared greatly"—using a Greek word combination that speaks of extreme alarm. It's exactly the same expression Matthew used to recount how the three disciples reacted on the Mount of Transfiguration when Christ's glory was unveiled (17:6). This kind of fear was a typical reaction of people who suddenly realized the truth about who Jesus is (cf. Mark 4:41; 5:33).

When the soldiers around the cross heard Jesus' exclamation, saw Him die, and then immediately felt the earthquake, it suddenly became all too clear to them that they had crucified the Son of God. They were stricken with terror. It wasn't merely the earthquake that they were afraid of. Rather they were terrified by the sudden realization that Jesus was innocent—and not *merely* innocent, but He was also precisely who He claimed to be. They had killed the Son of God. The centurion remembered the indictment of the Sanhedrin ("He made Himself the Son of God"—John 19:7), and having witnessed Jesus' death up close from beginning to end, he rendered his own verdict on the matter: "Truly this was the Son of God!"

The words were evidently a true expression of faith. Luke says, *"He glorified God,* saying, 'Certainly this was a righteous Man!'" (Luke 23:47, emphasis added). So the centurion and his soldiers with him were evidently the very first converts to Christ after His crucifixion, coming to faith at precisely the moment He expired.

THE DRAMA ENDED

John records that as the hour grew late, the Sanhedrin wanted the bodies off the crosses, so that they would not remain there overnight and defile the Sabbath. "Therefore, because it was the Preparation Day, that the bodies should not remain on the cross on the Sabbath (for that Sabbath was a high day), the Jews asked Pilate that their legs might be broken, and that they might be taken away" (John 19:31).

The Sabbath was a "high" Sabbath because it was the day after Passover, and therefore that particular Sabbath belonged to the Feast of Unleavened Bread. The Sanhedrin's pretentious reverence for the sacredness of the high Sabbath is ironic in light of how they were treating the Lord of the Sabbath Himself (cf. Mark 2:28). But it reveals again how they were wholly concerned merely for the appearance, and not the reality, of things. Old Testament law (Deuteronomy 21:23) strictly commanded that the body of anyone hanged on a tree be removed and buried out of sight, not left hanging all night. It is almost certain that most victims of Roman crucifixion were nonetheless left hanging on crosses for days. But this being Passover, it was an especially high Sabbath, so the Sanhedrin wanted the Jewish law observed. That is why they petitioned Pilate not to permit the bodies to remain on the crosses overnight. In order to keep their sanctimonious veneer intact, they now wanted Jesus to die, and die quickly.

As we noted on page 202, the breaking of the legs would make it certain that death would occur almost immediately, because once the legs could no longer push up to support the body's weight, the diaphragm would be severely constricted, and air could not be expelled. The victim would die of asphyxiation within minutes. The cruel practice also guaranteed that the victim died with as much pain as possible.

Soldiers from Pilate therefore came to the crucifixion site with the express purpose of breaking the victims' legs. John writes,

> Then the soldiers came and broke the legs of the first and of the other who was crucified with Him. But when they came to Jesus and saw that He was already dead, they did not break His legs. But one of the soldiers pierced His side with a spear, and immediately blood and water came out. And he who has seen has testified, and his testimony is true; and he knows that he is telling the truth, so that you may believe. For these things were done that the Scripture should be fulfilled, "Not one of His bones shall be broken." (19:32–36)

The legs of both criminals were broken. Within minutes, the forgiven thief was in Paradise with the Lord, who had preceded him to glory.

But the soldiers, finding Jesus already dead, decided not to break His bones. Instead, they pierced His side with a spear, to verify that He was dead. The blood and water that flowed out showed that He was. The watery fluid was probably excess serum that had collected in the pericardium (the membrane that encloses the heart). The blood was an indicator that the spear pierced the heart or aorta as well as the pericardium. The fact that blood and water came out separately from the same wound seems to indicate that death had occurred some period of time before the wound was inflicted, so that Christ's blood—even in the area of the heart—had already begun the process of coagulation.

Mark 15:43–44 says that after Jesus' death, Joseph of Arimathea came to ask Pilate for the body of Jesus, and "Pilate marveled that

He was already dead; and summoning the centurion, he asked him if He had been dead for some time." The relatively early hour at which Christ died surprised all those who were familiar with death by crucifixion. He died several hours before the typical crucifixion victim would have been expected to die. (Remember that crucifixion was designed to maximize the victim's pain while prolonging the process of dying.)

But Christ died at such an early hour in order to demonstrate what He had once told the Jewish leaders: "Therefore doth my Father love me, because I lay down my life, that I might take it again. No man taketh it from me, but I lay it down of myself. I have power to lay it down, and I have power to take it again. This commandment have I received of my Father" (John 10:17–18, KJV). He was sovereign, even over the timing of His own death.

Even the soldiers' failure to break His legs was a further fulfillment of Old Testament prophecy: "He guards all his bones; not one of them is broken" (Psalm 34:20). And thus from the beginning to the end of the crucifixion, Christ had remained sovereignly in charge. The Father's will had been fulfilled to the letter, and dozens of Old Testament prophecies were specifically fulfilled.

Christ was dead, but death had not conquered Him. On the first day of the week, He would burst forth triumphantly from the grave and show Himself alive to hundreds of eyewitnesses (1 Corinthians 15:5–8). He not only atoned for sin, but He demonstrated His Mastery over death in the process.

The resurrection of Christ was a divine stamp of approval on the atonement He purchased through His dying. Paul wrote that Jesus was "declared to be the Son of God with power according to the Spirit of holiness, by the resurrection from the dead" (Romans 1:4). The Resurrection therefore gave immediate, dramatic, and tangible proof of the efficacy of Christ's atoning death. The converse is true as well: It is the Cross, and what Jesus accomplished there, that gives the Resurrection its significance.

A thorough account of all the events and eyewitnesses surrounding Christ's resurrection would fill another entire volume, so it is not possible to examine the biblical narratives of the Resurrection here. (Perhaps one day, if the Lord permits, I will have the opportunity to publish such a volume.) But it's worth noting that the Resurrection is one of history's most carefully scrutinized and best-attested facts. The enemies of the gospel from the apostles' day until now have tried desperately to impeach the eyewitness testimony to Jesus' resurrection. They have not been able to do so, nor will they.

Still, it is vital to see that the early church's preaching focused as much on the *death* of Christ as on His *resurrection*. Paul wrote, "We preach Christ crucified" (1 Corinthians 1:23); "I determined not to know anything among you except Jesus Christ and Him crucified" (2:2); and, "God forbid that I should boast except in the cross of our Lord Jesus Christ" (Galatians 6:14).

Why did Paul place so much emphasis on the death of Christ, rather than always stressing the triumph of the Resurrection above even His death? Because, again, without the atoning work Christ did on the cross, His resurrection would be merely a wonder to stand back and admire. But it would have no personal ramifications for us. However, "if we died with Christ,"—that is, if He died in our place and in our stead—then "we believe that we shall also live with Him" (Romans 6:8). Because of the death he died, suffering the penalty of sin on our behalf, we become partakers with Him in His resurrection as well. That is virtually the whole point of Romans 6.

So don't ever pass over the meaning of the death of Christ on your way to celebrate the Resurrection. It is the Cross that gives meaning to the resurrection life. Only insofar as we are united with

Him in the likeness of His death, can we be certain of being raised with Him in the likeness of His resurrection (cf. Romans 6:5).

That is why "Jesus Christ and Him crucified" remains the very heart and soul of the gospel message. And in the words of the apostle Paul, every believer's deepest yearning should be this: "That I may know Him and the power of His resurrection, and the fellowship of His sufferings, being conformed to His death, if, by any means, I may attain to the resurrection from the dead" (Philippians 3:10–11).

❧ Index

The MacArthur Study Bible
John MacArthur, General Editor

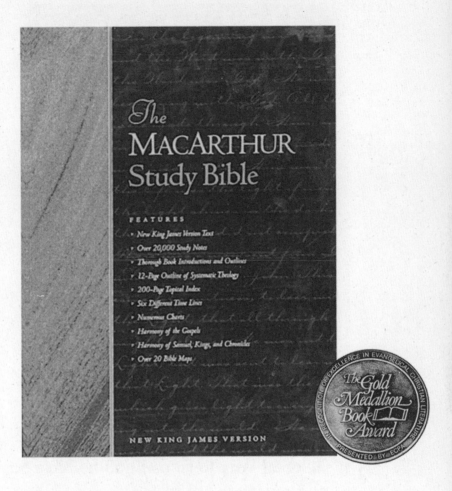

From the Moment You Pick It Up, You'll Know It Is a Classic

Featuring the word-for-word accuracy of the New King James Version, *The MacArthur Study Bible* is perfect for serious study. Pastor/teacher, John MacArthur, has compiled more than 20,000 study notes, a 200-page topical index, and numerous charts, maps, outlines and articles to create *The MacArthur Study Bible*. This Bible has been crafted with the finest materials in a variety of handsome bindings, including hardcover, indexed bonded leather, indexed genuine leather and Moroccan leather. Winner of "The 1998 Study Bible of the Year Award."

 WORD PUBLISHING

Available at Bookstores Everywhere.

www.wordpublishing.com

The MacArthur Topical Bible

John MacArthur, General Editor

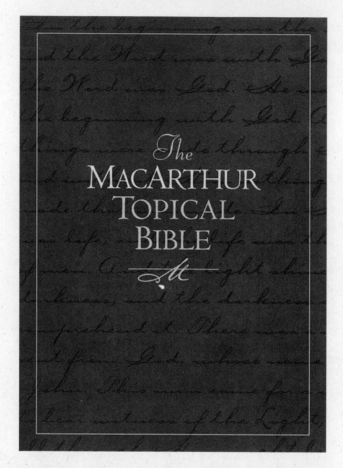

The Quickest Way to Find What the Bible Says
on Thousands of Life Topics and Ideas

In the excellent tradition of *Nave's Topical Bible,* this newly created reference book incorporates thousands of topics and ideas, traditional and contemporary, for believers today and in the new millennium. Carefully researched and prepared by Dr. John MacArthur and the staff of Grace To You, *The MacArthur Topical Bible* will quickly become the reference of choice of all serious Bible students. Using the New King James translation, this Bible is arranged alphabetically by topic and is completely cross-referenced. This exhaustive resource is an indispensable tool for the topical study of God's Word.

WORD PUBLISHING

Available at Bookstores Everywhere.

www.wordpublishing.com